ACKNOWLEDGMENTS

Thanks to Digital Union

CONTENTS

Historically, the traditional way to deliver business value was to identify your competitive advantage and set up a process to make that advantage sustainable. This model has been transformed through software. Marc Andreessen famously wrote an article for the Wall Street Journal titled "Software is Eating the World". This phrase helped shape a generation that thinks differently about IT. It encapsulates an important concept: there will not be a market in the world that will not be disrupted in some way by software. Over the past decade, there has been a shifting state of established market leaders from market dominance to extinction. Companies are now constantly challenged to compete at the pace of change of a startup, coupled with competing against the clout of "Internet scale." If you are not embracing technology to deliver value to your customers, then you are losing out to someone who is.

Market-disrupting companies differ from incumbents because they can repeatedly deliver software, with velocity, through iterative development cycles of short duration.

In every marketplace, speed wins. However, raw speed alone is insufficient. With speed alone, it is possible to run in circles or random directions and achieve very little. You need velocity. Velocity, as a vector quantity, is direction `aware. Direction is based on feedback. In another way, direction is dictated by what resonates with the customer. Speed must be coupled with the constant development-feedback cycle to ensure the Development-Feedback Cycle and progress in the right direction.

Digital Transformation & Feedback is essential for continually refining your product to resonate with user expectations. Speed coupled with the business alignment and feedback cycle produces velocity, and velocity is the only way to move both quickly and securely. Just development & Operation collaboration is not sufficient for the organization velocity.

It requires alignment of business and IT Strategy with good leadership transformation governance.

AAE model is one of the digital model which help to view the holistic digital transformation.

AAE model is to leverage technology & business for improved efficiency, innovation, and overall growth with principle of aligning on Awake(Pursuit of Strategy), Arise(Pursuit of Technology) and Enlight (Pursuit of Value)

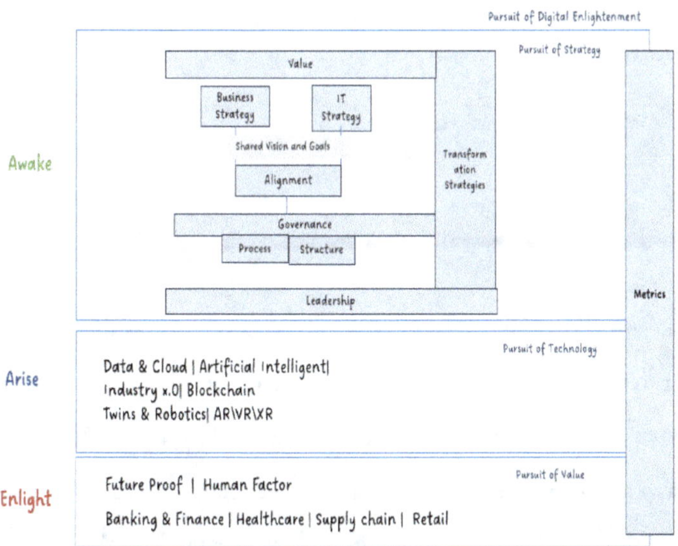

AAE Model

This conceptual framework provides a structured approach to navigating the dynamic landscape of business, technology, and value creation. Each step contributes to the overall journey of organizational growth, adaptation, and sustained success.

Here is the component of the AAE model.

Aware	Arise	Enlight
Enables individuals to adapt to emerging technologies, stay competitive, and thrive in an environment where digital fluency is increasingly essential.	Arise acquisition of knowledge in emerging fields is a pathway to unlocking countless opportunities and addressing complex challenges	Embracing this reality is not just a strategic imperative; it is a testament to the belief that, ultimately, the strength of any transformation lies in the hands, minds, and hearts of the people who drive it.
Business & IT Strategy Alignment Governance Digital & Agility Transformation Strategies Digital Leaders	Data & Cloud Artificial Intelligent Industry x.0 Blockchain Twins & Robotics AR\VR\XR	Future Proof Human Factor Banking & Finance Healthcare Supply chain Retail
We embark on this digitized journey, symbiotic relationship between digital and business strategies is not merely a technological imperative but a strategic necessity	catalyst for transformative societal progress. investment in human potential, a commitment to staying at the forefront of innovation, and a testament to our collective ability to shape a future where technology serves as a force for positive change. Embracing this journey is not merely a choice it is a responsibility to ourselves, to each other, and to the generations that will inherit the fruits of our technological curiosity and ingenuity.	enlightenment is not just a competitive advantage—it's a necessity for survival and sustained success. the success of any transformation is a human story—a narrative shaped by the collective will, resilience, and ingenuity of the individuals involved. it is a reminder that amidst the whirlwind of technological advancements and strategic shifts, the human factor remains the North Star, guiding organizations towards not just a transformed state but a more enlightened and empowered future

Awake Pursuit of Strategy:

"Embark on a strategic awakening in 'Awake Pursuit of Strategy' as we navigate the intersection of Business and IT Strategy Alignment, Governance Excellence, Digital & Agility, Transformation Strategies, and the essential qualities of Digital Leaders. Uncover the strategic framework that propels organizations toward success in an ever-evolving business landscape."

Business and IT Strategy Alignment:

- Define a clear understanding of the organization's business objectives and goals.

- Establish mechanisms to ensure that IT strategies align seamlessly with broader business strategies.

Governance Structure, Process, Leadership:

- Develop robust governance structures for effective decision-making and accountability.
- Define and refine organizational structures to facilitate collaboration between business and IT.
- Streamline processes to enhance efficiency and responsiveness.
- Foster leadership that promotes a culture of alignment, innovation, and continuous improvement.

Digital & agility:

- Explore the concept of digital agility and its role in responding to rapid technological changes.
- Discuss how organizations can cultivate a culture of digital agility.
- Highlight the benefits of being digitally agile, such as increased innovation and adaptability.

Transformation Strategies:

- Identify and implement transformation strategies to adapt to evolving business landscapes.
- Embrace change management practices to guide the organization through strategic transformations.

Digital Leaders:

- Outline essential leadership skills for the digital age.
- Discuss the importance of digital literacy and staying updated on technological trends.

◉ Provide guidance on developing leadership skills that foster a culture of innovation and continuous improvement.

Awakening Strategic Excellence:

"In 'Awake   Pursuit of Strategy,' we have journeyed through the intricacies of Business and IT Strategy Alignment, Governance Excellence, Digital & Agility, Transformation Strategies, and the quintessential traits of Digital Leaders. Join the pursuit of strategic excellence, where alignment, adaptability, and leadership converge to shape a future where organizations thrive in the wake of strategic awakenings."

"Embark on a transformative journey in 'Arise   Pursuit of Technology' as we delve into the cutting-edge realms of Artificial Intelligence (AI), Machine Learning (ML), Industry X.0 & Robotics, Blockchain, Twins & Robotics, and Augmented/Virtual/Mixed Reality (AR/VR/MR). Discover the opportunities, challenges, and the profound impact of these technologies on the evolving landscape of business and communication."

Artificial Intelligence (AI) and Machine Learning (ML)

- Explore diverse opportunities to harness the power of AI and ML for advanced data analysis, automation, and intelligent decision-making.
- Implement adaptive systems capable of learning and evolving in response to dynamic circumstances.
- Examine real-world applications where AI and ML are reshaping industries and driving innovation.

Industry X.0 & Robotics:

- Embrace the disruptive forces of Industry 4.0, integrating IoT, cloud computing, and advanced robotics to revolutionize operational processes.
- Illuminate the transformative potential of smart technologies in manufacturing, streamlining operations, and enhancing efficiency.

Blockchain

- ⚙ Investigate the robust applications of blockchain, revolutionizing transactional processes with security and transparency.
- ⚙ Explore how blockchain can elevate trust and efficiency across diverse business operations, creating a foundation for the future.

Twins & Robotics

- ⚙ Delve into the dynamic world of Twins & Robotics, exploring how they intertwine and amplify technological capabilities.
- ⚙ Uncover the potential of blockchain to fortify security in transactions and foster enhanced trust across various domains.

Augmented/Virtual/Mixed Reality (AR/VR/MR)

- ⚙ Grasp the implications of the metaverse for business and communication in the digital age.
- ⚙ Explore a multitude of opportunities, from virtual collaboration and immersive experiences to the emergence of novel business models within the AR/VR/MR spectrum.

Unveiling Tomorrow's Technological Landscape:

"In 'Arise   Pursuit of Technology,' we've uncovered the multifaceted tapestry of AI, ML, Industry X.0, Blockchain, Twins & Robotics, and Augmented/Virtual/Mixed Reality. Join the pursuit of technology as we unravel the vast potential and navigate the challenges, shaping a future where innovation, connectivity, and transformative technologies converge for the betterment of businesses and society."

Embark on an enlightening journey in 'Enlight Pursuit of Value' as we delve into the essential elements of Human Factor, Future-Proofing, Industry Domain Expertise, Value-Centric Decision-Making, and the practical applications of the AAE model in Banking & Finance, Healthcare, Supply Chain, and Retail.

Human Factor:

- Prioritize the well-being and professional development of employees.
- Foster a positive organizational culture that values diversity, inclusion, and employee engagement.

Future-Proofing:

- Anticipate future trends and technological advancements to stay ahead of the curve.
- Develop strategies to future-proof the organization against potential disruptions.

Industry Domain Expertise:

- Cultivate deep industry domain expertise to better understand market dynamics and customer needs.
- Align technological advancements with industry-specific requirements for maximum impact.

Value-Centric Decision-Making:

- Base decision-making on values such as integrity, sustainability, and social responsibility.
- Ensure that technology implementations contribute to the overall value proposition of the organization.

Recognize Industry Application of AAE Model:

- Explore the application of the AAE model in specific industries, including Banking & Finance, Healthcare, Supply Chain, and Retail.
- Highlight case studies and examples that demonstrate the effectiveness of the AAE model in these sectors.

Illuminating a Value-Driven Future:

"In 'Enlight Pursuit of Value,' we have navigated through the pillars of Human Factor, Future-Proofing, Industry Domain Expertise, Value-Centric Decision-Making, and the practical applications of the AAE model. Join the pursuit of value, where enlightened strategies, future readiness, industry expertise, and ethical decision-making converge to illuminate a future where organizations thrive, adapt, and contribute lasting value to society."

Overall Integration:

- Recognize that the three steps of Awake, Arise, and Enlight are interconnected and should be pursued in harmony.
- Foster a holistic approach where strategy, technology, and value creation reinforce and complement each other.

Awake: Pursuit of Strategy

Embark on a transformative journey of strategic enlightenment with 'Awake: Pursuit of Strategy.' Join us as we navigate the intricacies at the intersection of Business and IT Strategy Alignment, Governance Excellence, Digital & Agility, Transformation Strategies, and the essential qualities embodied by Digital Leaders. This unique exploration goes beyond the surface, delving deep into the strategic framework that propels organizations towards unprecedented success in an ever-evolving and dynamic business landscape.

In this strategic awakening, discover the nuanced dance between Business and IT Strategy Alignment, where the harmonious integration of these two critical elements becomes the linchpin for organizational success. Witness the unfolding of Governance Excellence, unraveling the layers of effective governance that lay the groundwork for resilient and sustainable operations.

Explore the vast landscape of Digital & Agility, where the synergy of digital technologies and the nimbleness of agile methodologies become essential pillars for organizations aiming to thrive in the digital era. Immerse yourself in the art and science of Transformation Strategies, uncovering the methodologies and approaches that propel organizations from their current state to a future-ready and adaptive state.

Moreover, 'Awake' delves into the qualities that define Digital Leaders, shedding light on the indispensable traits and skills that visionary leaders possess in steering organizations through the complexities of the modern business environment.

In 'Awake: Pursuit of Strategy,' the pursuit is not just a journey; it's a strategic awakening that equips individuals and organizations with the insights and tools needed to navigate the strategic landscape successfully. Prepare to awaken your strategic prowess and chart a course toward a future of strategic excellence.

In fast-paced technology-driven world, the alignment between business and IT strategies has become crucial for organizations seeking to stay competitive and achieve their goals. Business & IT Strategy Alignment refers to the process of synchronizing the objectives, priorities, and activities of the business and IT departments to ensure a seamless integration and mutual support. This alignment enables organizations to optimize their operations, enhance customer satisfaction, and drive innovation.

Understanding Alignment:

To embark on the journey of Business & IT Strategy Alignment, it is essential to first understand the concept and its significance. Alignment ensures that IT initiatives are closely aligned with the overall business objectives, enabling organizations to leverage technology as a strategic enabler rather than just a support function. It fosters collaboration, improves decision-making, and enhances the organization's ability to adapt to changing market dynamics.

Developing a Framework:

Creating a robust framework is crucial for successful Business & IT Strategy Alignment. This framework should encompass a clear vision, well-defined goals, and a roadmap to achieve them. It should involve key stakeholders from both the business and IT departments, including executives, managers, and subject matter experts, to ensure a comprehensive perspective.

Creating a Shared Vision:

Aligning business and IT strategies requires a shared vision that outlines the desired outcomes and the path to achieve them. This shared vision should be developed collaboratively, ensuring that both business and IT departments have a common understanding of the organization's goals and objectives. Regular communication and feedback loops play a vital role in maintaining alignment and fostering a sense of ownership among all stakeholders.

Aligning Processes and Systems:

Identifying gaps and inefficiencies in existing processes and systems is a crucial step in achieving Business & IT Strategy Alignment. Conducting process audits can help identify areas for improvement and opportunities for automation or optimization. By aligning processes and systems, organizations can eliminate silos, reduce redundancy, and enhance efficiency across the board. Implementing enterprise-wide solutions, such as integrated software platforms or cloud-based systems, can further streamline operations and facilitate collaboration.

Building an Agile IT Organization:

In an ever-evolving business landscape, agility is key to success. Organizations should embrace agile methodologies and foster a culture of continuous improvement within their IT departments. Adopting agile practices, such as Scrum or Kanban, can enhance collaboration, increase flexibility, and accelerate project delivery. Encouraging a mindset of experimentation, learning, and adaptation enables IT teams to respond swiftly to changing business needs, ensuring ongoing alignment between business and IT strategies.

Measuring and Monitoring Alignment:

Establishing metrics and tracking key performance indicators (KPIs) is crucial to measure the effectiveness of Business & IT Strategy Alignment efforts. These metrics should align with the organization's goals and provide insights into the impact of IT initiatives on overall business performance. Regular monitoring and reporting enable organizations to identify deviations, make informed decisions, and take corrective actions promptly.

Overcoming Challenges:

Aligning business and IT strategies is not without its challenges. Cultural differences, resistance to change, and lack of communication can hinder the alignment process. Organizations should invest in change management initiatives to address these challenges effectively. Promoting a culture of transparency, fostering open communication channels, and providing training and support to employees can help overcome resistance and facilitate a smooth alignment process.

Achieving Business & IT Strategy Alignment is a continuous journey that requires commitment, collaboration, and adaptability. By understanding the importance of alignment, creating a shared vision, aligning processes and systems, building an agile IT organization, and measuring and monitoring alignment, organizations can unlock the potential benefits of integrating their business and IT strategies.

Successful alignment leads to improved operational efficiency, enhanced customer satisfaction, and increased innovation, positioning organizations for long-term success in today's dynamic business landscape.

In the intricate dance between business strategy and information technology, organizations often find themselves grappling with the challenge of synchronization. The complexities of both domains demand a structured approach, and this is where frameworks come into play. Chapter 5 explores various frameworks that serve as guideposts for achieving seamless alignment between business and IT strategies.

Business & IT Alignment Canvas

The intricate dance between business and IT functions has given rise to a strategic tool that acts as a guiding framework, fostering collaboration, clarity, and effective decision-making — the Business & IT Alignment Canvas.

This canvas is more than just a visual representation; it is a dynamic blueprint that encapsulates the delicate balance between business aspirations and the technological prowess required to turn those aspirations into reality. By providing a structured canvas, organizations gain a powerful means to articulate, visualize, and strategize the alignment of their business goals with the capabilities of their IT infrastructure.

The Business & IT Alignment Canvas serves as a comprehensive map, helping stakeholders navigate the complex terrain of aligning business and IT strategies. From defining clear objectives and identifying key stakeholders to delineating IT capabilities and aligning technological roadmaps with business milestones, the canvas offers a holistic view that facilitates informed decision-making and ensures that every technological endeavor is intricately woven into the fabric of the organization's overarching strategy.

Business & IT Alignment Canvas

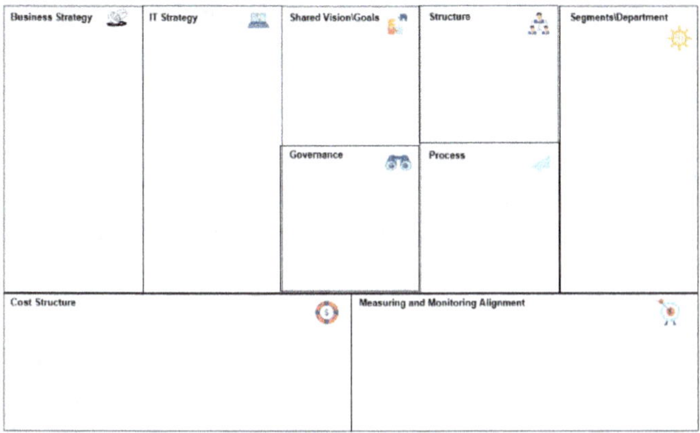

Let's delve deeper into each section of the Business and IT Alignment Canvas, providing more details and suggesting questions to ask:

Business Strategy:

Define the high-level goals, objectives, and competitive positioning of the business.

Questions to Ask

- What are the primary business objectives for the next 1-3 years?
- How does the business differentiate itself in the market?
- What market trends and customer needs are influencing the business strategy?

IT Strategy:

Outline the technology initiatives and plans that support the business strategy.

Questions to Ask

- How does the IT strategy align with and support the business strategy?
- What key technology initiatives are planned to enhance business capabilities?
- How will IT contribute to digital transformation efforts?

Shared Vision and Goals:

Articulate a common vision and identify specific goals that align business and IT efforts.

Questions to Ask

- What is the shared vision that both business and IT aim to achieve?
- What are the common goals that contribute to the success of the organization?
- How are these goals communicated and understood across the organization?

Structure:

Describe the organizational structure, emphasizing alignment between business and IT.

Questions to Ask

- How is the organization structured to facilitate collaboration between business and IT?
- What reporting lines exist to ensure effective communication and decision-making?
- Are there cross-functional teams or roles that bridge the gap between

business and IT?

Break down the organization into segments or departments, defining their roles and responsibilities.

Questions to Ask

- What are the key responsibilities of each department or segment?
- How do business units and IT functions collaborate to achieve common goals?
- Are there specific projects or initiatives that require cross-functional collaboration?

Establish governance mechanisms for decision-making and accountability.

Questions to Ask

- How are decisions related to business and IT made within the organization?
- What governance structures exist to ensure alignment and accountability?
- Are there regular forums for business and IT leaders to discuss strategic alignment?

Document key business and IT processes, identifying areas for integration and collaboration.

Questions to Ask

- What are the critical business processes that require IT support?
- How are business and IT processes aligned to enhance operational efficiency?

- Are there opportunities for process improvements or automation?

Cost Structure:

Break down the cost structure related to both business and IT activities.

Questions to Ask

- What are the major costs associated with business operations and IT initiatives?
- How do IT investments contribute to achieving business objectives?
- Are there opportunities to optimize costs while maintaining alignment?

Measuring and Monitoring Alignment:

Define metrics and KPIs to measure the effectiveness of business and IT alignment.

Questions to Ask

- What key performance indicators are used to measure alignment?
- How often are alignment metrics reviewed, and by whom?
- What actions are taken based on the results of alignment assessments?

Additional Tips:

- Foster an open dialogue and encourage feedback during the canvas creation process.
- Ensure representation from both business and IT stakeholders to capture diverse perspectives.
- Use the canvas as a dynamic tool, revisiting and updating it regularly to reflect changes in strategies and priorities.

By addressing these details and asking relevant questions, you can create a comprehensive Business and IT Alignment Canvas that serves as a valuable tool for fostering collaboration and ensuring the ongoing alignment of business and IT strategies.

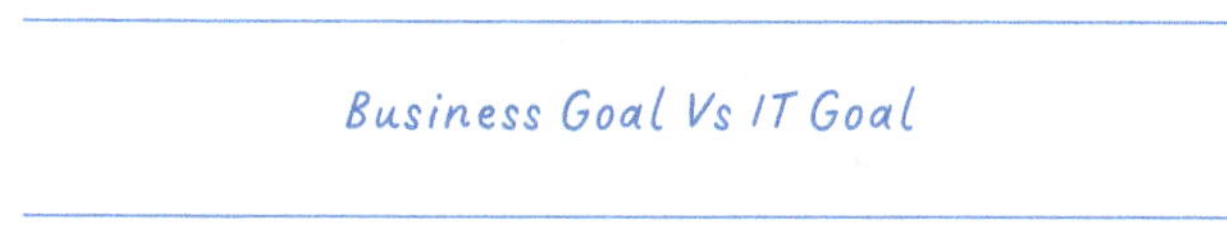

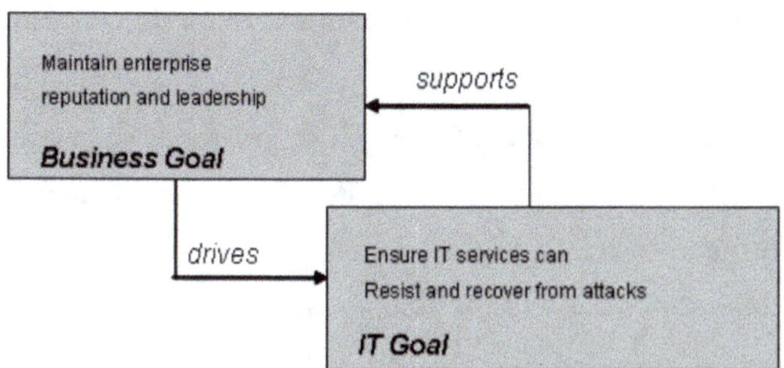

The relationship between business goals and IT goals is symbiotic. Business goals drive IT goals, while IT goals support business goals.

Business goals are the overall objectives that an organization wants to achieve. They are typically high-level and strategic, and they may include objectives such as increasing revenue, reducing costs, or improving customer satisfaction.

IT goals are the specific IT objectives that are necessary to achieve t business goals. They are typically more detailed and operational, and they may include objectives such as developing new software systems, improving network security, or enhancing data analytics capabilities.

There are a number of ways in which business goals can drive IT goals:

- Businesses can articulate their strategic goals and objectives to their

IT organizations. This ensures that IT is aligned with the overall business direction and that IT investments are focused on supporting key business initiatives.

- Businesses can provide IT with clear performance metrics and targets. This allows IT to measure its success in achieving business goals and to make adjustments as needed.
- Businesses can encourage collaboration between IT and business units. This fosters communication and understanding between the two groups, which can lead to more effective IT solutions.

IT can also play a key role in supporting business goals by:

- Developing and implementing new technologies that can help businesses to achieve their objectives.
- Improving the efficiency and effectiveness of business processes.
- Collecting and analyzing data that can be used to make better business decisions.
- Protecting business-critical data and systems from security threats.

- Increased business agility and responsiveness to market changes.
- Enhanced customer satisfaction and loyalty.
- Improved operational efficiency and cost savings.
- To achieve this alignment, businesses and IT organizations need to have open and ongoing communication, and they need to work together to ensure that IT investments are aligned with business objectives.

Relationship between business goals and IT goals:

Business Goal	IT Goal
Increase revenue	Develop new sales and marketing campaigns.
Reduce costs	Implement automation and cloud-based solutions.
Improve customer satisfaction	Provide personalized customer experiences.
Enhance operational efficiency	Streamline business processes and automate tasks.
Protect sensitive data	Implement strong security measures and data governance policies.

Digital Pathways

Managing Organizational Explosions During Digital Business Transformations

Figure 1: Four Digital Transformation Pathways

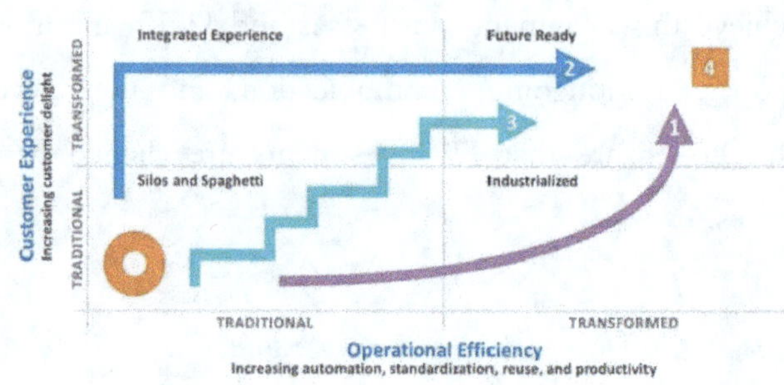

Research identified four transformation pathways (summarized in Figure 1) that companies take to break free of the silos and complexity and prepare themselves for the future. Pathway 1 focuses on addressing the operational complexity through digital industrialization and standardization, which makes it easier to improve the customer experience by reusing modular business capabilities. Companies following this pathway ultimately have the best financial performance, but it can take years to build reusable capabilities and the customer experience. Meanwhile, existing competitors and disruptive new entrants may force a company to take one of the other transformation pathways.5 Companies may first need to focus on customer initiatives by creating integrated, well designed user experiences and offerings while hiding their operational complexity (Pathway 2). Alternatively, they could follow Pathway 3 and attempt to address both their operational and customer experience capabilities iteratively. Or they could choose not to transform the current organization but instead follow Pathway 4, which means they would create a new future-ready company or subsidiary that isn't burdened with legacy processes and systems

Digital mastery maturity

Digital mastery maturity refers to the level of proficiency and sophistication an organization has attained in leveraging digital technologies to achieve its business objectives. Organizations progress through different stages of digital maturity, and their ability to effectively navigate and capitalize on digital advancements often determines their competitive advantage. Various frameworks and models exist to assess digital maturity. One such model is the Digital Maturity Model, which typically consists of several maturity levels. Here is a simplified representation:

Level 1: Initiating

Characteristics:
- Limited digital presence.
- Ad-hoc use of digital technologies.
- Basic awareness of digital trends.

Focus Areas:

- Establishing a foundational understanding of digital technologies.
- Experimenting with digital initiatives.

Level 2: Experimenting

Characteristics:

- Increased experimentation with digital tools and strategies.
- Initiatives are often siloed and department-specific.
- Limited coordination across the organization.

Focus Areas:

- Piloting digital projects and assessing their impact.
- Building a digital culture within individual teams.

Level 3: Scaling

Characteristics:

- Successful digital initiatives are identified and scaled.
- Increased collaboration between departments.
- Growing awareness of the importance of digital transformation.

Focus Areas:

- Expanding the scope of successful digital projects.
- Integrating digital initiatives into core business functions.
- Developing digital skills across the organization.

Level 4: Optimizing

Characteristics:

- Digital technologies are embedded in core business processes.
- Data-driven decision-making is prevalent.
- Cross-functional collaboration is the norm.

Focus Areas:

- Continuous improvement of existing digital capabilities.
- Harnessing data analytics for strategic decision-making.
- Developing a proactive approach to emerging technologies.

Level 5: Innovating

Characteristics:

- Continuous innovation is part of the organizational DNA.
- Agile and adaptive to market changes.
- Strong external partnerships for innovation.

Focus Areas:

- Encouraging a culture of innovation and experimentation.
- Embracing emerging technologies for competitive advantage.

Level 6: Transforming

Characteristics:

- Digital is integrated into the organization's strategic vision.
- Business model transformation is ongoing.
- Leadership actively champions digital initiatives.

Focus Areas:

- Transforming the entire business model to be digitally native.
- Fostering a culture of continuous transformation.

The specific stages and characteristics may vary depending on the model used, but the essence remains consistent: as organizations progress through higher levels of digital maturity, they become more adept at leveraging digital technologies strategically, transforming their operations, and driving innovation for sustained success in the digital era. The journey towards digital mastery is dynamic, requiring ongoing adaptation to technological advancements and changing market landscape.

Governance

Introduction:

In digital era, the alignment between business and IT strategies has become crucial for organizations to thrive and stay competitive. However, achieving this alignment is not without its challenges. Cultural differences, resistance to change, lack of communication, and resource constraints often hinder the efforts to bridge the gap between these two critical areas. To overcome these hurdles and unlock the full potential of technology, organizations need to implement effective governance frameworks that promote transparency, accountability, and strategic alignment. We will delve into the realm of IT governance and business governance, exploring their importance and providing insights into their implementation.

Understanding IT Governance:

IT governance is a framework that ensures IT investments support business objectives and helps organizations navigate the complex digital landscape. It encompasses various domains, including value delivery, strategic alignment, performance management, resource management, and risk management . By establishing clear policies, procedures, and decision-making processes, IT governance enables organizations to optimize their IT resources and align them with business strategies. It also enhances transparency and accountability, ensuring compliance with legal and regulatory requirements

The Role of Business Governance:

Business governance, on the other hand, focuses on the overall management and direction of the organization. It involves the establishment of a competent board of directors, defining roles and responsibilities, and promoting transparency and accountability at all levels. Business governance ensures that the interests of shareholders, stakeholders, and the public are protected, and that the organization operates ethically and responsibly.

The Synergy between IT Governance and Business Governance:

Achieving alignment between IT and business strategies requires a harmonious relationship between IT governance and business governance. Both frameworks should work in tandem to drive organizational performance and success. Effective communication, collaboration, and stakeholder engagement are crucial to bridge the gap between IT and business leaders [3]. By involving key stakeholders and decision-makers from both sides, organizations can foster a shared vision and ensure that technology investments are aligned with strategic objectives.

Risks Associated with IT Investments:

Investing in IT projects and initiatives involves inherent risks. These risks include financial risks, such as cost overruns and budget constraints, as well as technical risks, such as system failures and security breaches. To mitigate these risks, organizations must implement robust risk management practices and adhere to industry standards and best practices .By conducting thorough risk assessments, organizations can identify

.potential vulnerabilities and implement appropriate measures to protect their investments.

Managing and Protecting Information Assets:

Information is a valuable asset for organizations, and its management and protection are critical for business continuity and success. Information governance ensures that information is properly managed, protected, and used in a compliant and ethical manner. It involves establishing policies, procedures, and controls to govern the creation, storage, access, and disposal of information assets [2]. By implementing effective information governance practices, organizations can reduce the risk of data breaches, ensure data integrity, and enhance decision-making processes.

IT security

IT security is important in governance because it plays a crucial role in protecting an organization's sensitive information, systems, and assets. Here's why:

Risk mitigation: IT security governance helps identify and assess potential risks and vulnerabilities in the organization's IT infrastructure. By implementing appropriate security measures, organizations can effectively mitigate these risks and prevent security breaches or unauthorized access to data.

Decision-making: IT security governance establishes clear roles and responsibilities for decision-making regarding IT security. This ensures that authorized individuals make informed decisions to protect the organization's information assets, aligning them with business objectives and compliance requirements.

Accountability: IT security governance promotes accountability by defining the responsibilities of different stakeholders involved in managing IT security. This includes assigning accountability for incident response, compliance, and ongoing monitoring of security controls.

Transparency: IT security governance ensures transparency by establishing processes and mechanisms for reporting and communicating IT security-related matters. This helps stakeholders, including shareholders, stakeholders, and the public, understand the organization's security posture and the measures taken to protect their interests.

Overall, IT security governance is crucial for organizations to proactively manage risks, protect sensitive information, and ensure the integrity, availability, and confidentiality of their IT systems and data. It aligns IT security strategies with business objectives and compliance requirements, enabling organizations to operate securely and maintain trust with their stakeholders.

The key principles of IT governance are essential for effective implementation and continuous improvement. These principles include:

Clear Roles and Responsibilities: Clearly defining the roles and responsibilities of individuals and teams involved in IT governance ensures accountability and promotes effective decision-making.

Alignment with Business Objectives: IT governance should be aligned with the organization's overall business objectives and strategy to ensure that IT investments and initiatives support the achievement of these goals.

Risk Management: Implementing risk management processes and practices helps identify and mitigate potential IT risks, ensuring the security and resilience of IT systems and data.

Compliance: IT governance should ensure compliance with relevant laws, regulations, and industry standards to protect sensitive information and maintain trust with stakeholders.

Performance Measurement: Establishing metrics and performance indicators allows organizations to assess the effectiveness of IT governance practices and make informed decisions for improvement.

Continuous Improvement: IT governance should be a dynamic process, continuously monitoring and adapting to changes in technology, business needs, and emerging threats.

These principles guide organizations in establishing a robust IT governance framework that supports the effective management of IT resources, enhances decision-making, and mitigates IT-related risks

---

Understanding Frameworks

Frameworks provide a systematic structure for organizations to organize, plan, and execute their business and IT strategies cohesively. They act as blueprints, offering a set of best practices, principles, and guidelines that help navigate the intricate landscape of alignment. Understanding the nuances of these frameworks is paramount to their effective implementation.

COBIT (Control Objectives for Information and Related Technologies)

COBIT, developed by ISACA, is a globally recognized framework that focuses on aligning IT with business goals. It provides a comprehensive set of controls and processes, ensuring that IT activities support the organization's objectives. From strategic planning to risk management,

COBIT offers a holistic approach to business and IT alignment.

Example: A multinational corporation utilizes COBIT to establish standardized processes for IT governance, ensuring that each business unit adheres to a unified set of principles.

ITIL (Information Technology Infrastructure Library)

ITIL is a set of practices that focuses on aligning IT services with the needs of the business. By emphasizing service delivery, ITIL helps organizations enhance customer satisfaction and optimize costs. This framework is particularly beneficial in defining processes that ensure IT services are aligned with business requirements.

Example: An e-commerce company adopts ITIL to streamline its service management processes, resulting in improved service quality and faster response times to customer needs.

TOGAF (The Open Group Architecture Framework)

TOGAF is an enterprise architecture methodology that aids in organizing and executing business processes to improve efficiency. It focuses on creating a standardized approach to the design, planning, implementation, and governance of an enterprise's information architecture.

Example: A financial institution adopts TOGAF to create a unified architecture, ensuring that IT systems align with business objectives while adhering to regulatory requirements

Tailoring Frameworks to Fit

No one-size-fits-all solution exists when it comes to frameworks. Organizations must tailor these methodologies to suit their unique cultures, goals, and challenges. The success of implementing a framework lies not just in adherence but in the adaptability to the specific needs of the organization.

Example: A healthcare organization integrates elements of COBIT and ITIL, customizing the framework to accommodate both regulatory compliance and the need for seamless service delivery.

The Roadmap to Implementation

Frameworks are not magic bullets; their effectiveness relies on meticulous planning and execution. This section of the chapter provides a step-by-step guide to implementing chosen frameworks, including stakeholder engagement, training programs, and continuous improvement processes.

Example: An educational institution embarks on a phased implementation of ITIL, starting with training programs for IT staff and gradually extending the framework to other departments, resulting in a more streamlined and responsive IT service.

Pitfalls and Challenges

While frameworks offer invaluable guidance, they are not immune to pitfalls. This section addresses common challenges faced during implementation, such as resistance to change, resource constraints, and the need for continuous adaptation.

Example: A manufacturing company encounters resistance from employees accustomed to existing processes during the implementation of COBIT. Through effective change management and communication strategies, the organization successfully navigates these challenges.

Emphasizing that frameworks are tools, not solutions in themselves. When wielded with precision and adapted thoughtfully, they become powerful instruments for achieving business and IT strategy alignment. Organizations must view these frameworks as enablers, fostering an environment where the synergy between business and IT thrives, propelling the organization toward sustained success.

Enterprise governance is a broad concept that encompasses the structures, processes, and people responsible for ensuring that an organization achieves its strategic objectives. It is concerned with defining and maintaining a framework of rules, policies, and procedures that guide the organization's activities and ensure that it operates in a responsible, ethical, and compliant manner.

Key Components of Enterprise Governance

Enterprise governance can be divided into several key components:

Strategic governance: This focuses on ensuring that the organization's strategic direction is aligned with its overall objectives and that resources are allocated effectively to achieve those objectives.

Operational governance: This focuses on ensuring that the organization's daily operations are conducted efficiently and effectively, and that risks are managed appropriately.

Risk governance: This focuses on identifying, assessing, and managing risks to the organization, including financial, operational, and reputational risks.

Compliance governance: This focuses on ensuring that the organization complies with all applicable laws, regulations, and industry standards.

Performance governance: This focuses on measuring and reporting on the organization's performance against its strategic objectives, and taking corrective action as needed.

Benefits of Enterprise Governance

There are many benefits to implementing effective enterprise governance, including:

Increased strategic alignment: Enterprise governance helps to ensure that the organization's activities are aligned with its strategic objectives, which can lead to improved decision-making and better performance.

Reduced risk: Enterprise governance helps to identify and mitigate potential risks, which can protect the organization from financial losses, reputational damage, and legal liability.

Improved efficiency: Enterprise governance can help to streamline processes, reduce waste, and improve overall efficiency.

Enhanced accountability: Enterprise governance helps to ensure that everyone in the organization is accountable for their actions, which can lead to a more responsible and ethical culture.

Increased stakeholder trust: Enterprise governance can help to build trust with stakeholders, such as investors, customers, and employees.

Challenges of Enterprise Governance

While there are many benefits to implementing enterprise governance, there are also some challenges that organizations need to be aware of:

Cost: Implementing enterprise governance can be costly, as it requires investment in people, processes, and technology.

Cultural change: Implementing enterprise governance may require a change in organizational culture, as people may need to be more willing to share information and comply with new rules and procedures.

Sustainability: Ensuring that enterprise governance is sustainable over time can be challenging, as it requires ongoing commitment and effort from all levels of the organization.

Best Practices for Enterprise Governance

There are a number of best practices that organizations can follow to implement effective enterprise governance:

Establish clear governance objectives: Define the specific objectives that you want to achieve through enterprise governance.

Design a governance framework: Create a governance framework that outlines the roles, responsibilities, and processes for managing enterprise risk and ensuring compliance.

Implement effective risk management practices: Identify, assess, and manage potential risks to the organization.

Establish clear communication channels: Ensure that there are clear communication channels between different parts of the organization and with stakeholders.

Develop a culture of accountability: Foster a culture of accountability where people are held responsible for their actions.

Regularly review and update your governance framework: As the organization's business and environment evolves, the governance framework should be reviewed and updated as needed.

Conclusion

Enterprise governance is an essential component of any organization that wants to achieve its strategic objectives and operate in a responsible and ethical manner. By implementing effective enterprise governance, organizations can improve their decision-making, reduce risk, increase efficiency, enhance accountability, and build trust with stakeholders.

Enterprise governance refers to the framework and processes that organizations put in place to ensure effective decision-making, accountability, and risk management at the highest level. It encompasses various aspects, including corporate governance, IT governance, and information governance.

Corporate governance focuses on the overall management and control of the organization, ensuring that the interests of shareholders, stakeholders, and the public are protected. It involves establishing a competent board of directors, defining roles and responsibilities, and promoting transparency and accountability.

IT governance, on the other hand, is concerned with aligning IT strategies and initiatives with the overall business objectives. It involves decision-making processes, policies, and structures that ensure IT investments are prioritized, risks are managed effectively, and IT resources are utilized efficiently.

Information governance is a critical component of enterprise governance, aiming to ensure that information is managed effectively, compliant with regulations, and used strategically to achieve business goals. It involves policies, procedures, and technologies for information management, data quality, privacy, and security.

By implementing enterprise governance practices, organizations can achieve several benefits, including improved decision-making, enhanced accountability, increased transparency, and reduced risks. It enables organizations to align their business, IT, and information strategies, leading to better operational efficiency, customer satisfaction, and overall performance.

How much governance needed ?

The amount of governance needed for IT and business alignment depends on various factors, including the size and complexity of the organization, industry regulations, the nature of IT systems, and the criticality of IT to business operations. While there is no one-size-fits-all answer, here are some considerations to help determine the appropriate level of governance:

Organizational Size and Complexity

Larger and more complex organizations typically require a more robust governance structure. This may involve establishing governance committees, defining decision-making processes, and ensuring clear lines of communication between business and IT.

Industry Regulations

Industries with strict regulations, such as finance, healthcare, or government, often require higher levels of governance to ensure compliance. Governance mechanisms may need to address security, privacy, and data protection concerns.

Strategic Importance of IT

If IT plays a critical role in achieving business objectives and maintaining a competitive advantage, a higher level of governance is usually necessary. This includes governance over IT strategy, investments, and project delivery.

Risk Tolerance

Organizations with lower risk tolerance may opt for a more

stringent governance framework to mitigate risks associated with IT projects and operations. This may involve thorough risk assessments and compliance checks.

IT Project Portfolio

The number and complexity of IT projects in an organization's portfolio can influence the need for governance. A diverse project portfolio may require different levels of oversight and coordination.

Alignment Challenges

If there are historical or ongoing challenges in aligning IT with business goals, increased governance may be necessary to enhance communication, decision-making, and collaboration.

Decision-Making Complexity

The complexity of decisions related to IT investments, projects, and operations can impact the governance needed. Critical decisions may require input from both business and IT leadership.

Collaboration Requirements

The degree of collaboration required between business and IT functions can influence the need for governance. Collaborative governance structures ensure that decisions are made with input from both sides.

Change Management Needs

Organizations undergoing significant changes, such as digital transformations, may require heightened governance to manage the impact on both business and IT processes.

Continuous Improvement

Establishing governance mechanisms for continuous improvement ensures that the alignment between IT and business remains effective over time. Regular reviews and adjustments may be needed.

It's essential to strike a balance between having enough governance to ensure alignment and avoid risks while avoiding excessive bureaucracy that could hinder agility. Regular assessments of the effectiveness of governance mechanisms and adjustments based on changing organizational needs are critical. Tailor the governance model to suit the specific characteristics and requirements of your organization.

There are a number of ways to quantify the digitalization in an enterprise. Some common metrics include:

Percentage of digital revenue: This metric measures the proportion of total revenue that is generated from digital channels, such as online sales, mobile apps, and digital advertising.

Number of digital customers: This metric tracks the number of customers who engage with the company through digital channels. This can include customers who purchase products or services online, use mobile apps, or interact with the company on social media.

Percentage of employees who use digital tools: This metric measures the proportion of employees who use digital tools to perform their jobs. This can include productivity software, collaboration tools, and learning platforms.

Percentage of business processes that are digitalized: This metric measures the proportion of business processes that have been automated or streamlined using digital technology. This can include order processing, customer service, and procurement.

Percentage of data that is digitized: This metric measures the proportion of data that is stored and processed in digital format. This includes customer data, financial data, and operational data.

Percentage of revenue from digital products and services: This metric measures the proportion of total revenue that is generated from digital products and services. This can include software, cloud computing, and digital advertising.

Return on investment (ROI) from digital initiatives: This metric measures the financial benefit of digital initiatives compared to their cost. This can be calculated by dividing the net profit from digital initiatives by the total cost of digital investments.

In addition to these quantitative metrics, it is also important to consider qualitative factors when quantifying digitalization. These factors can include:

The maturity of the organization's digital capabilities: This refers to the level of expertise and experience that the organization has in developing and deploying digital solutions.

The culture of innovation and experimentation: This refers to the organization's willingness to try new things and take risks in order to improve their digital offerings.

The alignment of digital initiatives with business strategy: This refers to the extent to which digital initiatives are aligned with the organization's overall business goals.

By measuring both quantitative and qualitative factors, organizations can gain a comprehensive understanding of their digitalization progress and identify areas for improvement.

Digital & Agility

Digital and agile transformations are often interconnected and complementary initiatives that organizations undertake to navigate the complexities of the modern business landscape. Combining these two transformations creates a holistic approach to achieving strategic objectives, fostering innovation, and staying responsive to rapidly changing market conditions. Here's an integrated perspective on digital and agile transformation:

Strategic Alignment

Digital Transformation: Focuses on aligning digital initiatives with overall business strategy. This involves leveraging technology to achieve strategic goals, enhance operational efficiency, and create new opportunities.

Agile Transformation: Ensures that the organization's values, principles, and practices align with its strategic objectives. Agile methodologies are applied not only in development but across various business functions.

Customer-Centricity:

Digital Transformation: Emphasizes understanding and meeting customer expectations by leveraging digital tools, data analytics, and personalized experiences.

Agile Transformation: Prioritizes customer collaboration, frequent feedback, and iterative development to ensure that the end product aligns closely with customer needs.

Cultural Shift:

Digital Transformation: Involves a cultural shift toward embracing digital technologies, data-driven decision-making, and a proactive approach to innovation.

Agile Transformation: Requires a cultural shift toward collaboration, transparency, adaptability, and continuous improvement. This includes breaking down silos and fostering a culture of experimentation.

Flexibility and Adaptability:

Digital Transformation: Focuses on creating a technology infrastructure that is flexible, scalable, and able to adapt to evolving business requirements.

Agile Transformation: Embeds agility in processes and structures, allowing the organization to respond rapidly to changes in the market, customer feedback, or internal dynamics.

Technology Integration:

Digital Transformation: Involves the integration of advanced technologies such as artificial intelligence, machine learning, the Internet of Things, and cloud computing.

Agile Transformation: Encompasses the use of agile methodologies like Scrum or Kanban to manage and deliver technology projects in an iterative and incremental manner.

Digital Transformation: Encourages a culture of continuous learning to stay abreast of technological advancements and industry trends.

Agile Transformation: Ingrains a mindset of continuous improvement through regular retrospectives, feedback loops, and adapting processes based on lessons learned.

Digital Transformation: Often requires collaboration between IT and business units to ensure technology solutions align with business objectives.

Agile Transformation: Promotes cross-functional collaboration by bringing together individuals with diverse skills and perspectives to work collaboratively on projects.

Digital Transformation: Empowers teams with digital tools and technologies to enhance productivity and efficiency.

Agile Transformation: Empowers teams to make decisions, self-organize, and continuously deliver value, fostering a sense of ownership.

Digital Transformation: Focuses on achieving specific business outcomes, whether it's increased revenue, improved customer satisfaction, or operational excellence.

Agile Transformation: Prioritizes delivering value to customers through working solutions, placing an emphasis on outcomes rather than just outputs.

In essence, the integration of digital and agile transformation acknowledges that technology alone is not enough; a flexible, adaptive, and collaborative approach is essential to capitalize on the opportunities presented by digital advancements. This integrated transformation enables organizations to not only digitize their processes but also to build a culture and structure that thrives in a rapidly changing environment.

Transformation Strategies

While consulting companies may not explicitly label their strategies as distinct types of digital transformation, they often provide frameworks and methodologies that encompass various aspects of digital transformation. Here are some examples from top consulting companies:

McKinsey & Company: Digital Quotient (DQ):

McKinsey's Digital Quotient is a framework that assesses an organization's digital maturity across various dimensions, including strategy, capabilities, and culture. It helps organizations understand their current digital standing and identifies areas for improvement.

Deloitte: Digital Transformation Framework:

Deloitte's digital transformation framework involves a holistic approach that encompasses strategy, operations, technology, and talent. It emphasizes the need for organizations to align digital initiatives with business objectives and create a culture of continuous innovation.

Accenture's Industry X.

Accenture's Industry X.0 focuses on the intersection of industry and digital technologies. It helps organizations leverage technologies like IoT, AI, and analytics to transform their core operations and business models.

BCG: Digital Acceleration Index (DAI)

Boston Consulting Group's Digital Acceleration Index helps organizations evaluate their digital capabilities and identify areas for improvement. It assesses an organization's readiness to digitally transform and provides a roadmap for acceleration.

PwC's Digital Fitness

PwC's Digital Fitness aims to assess and enhance the digital skills and capabilities of an organization's workforce. It focuses on building a digitally fluent culture and workforce to drive successful digital transformation.

Capgemini's Digital Mastery Model

Capgemini's Digital Mastery Model evaluates an organization's digital maturity across five dimensions: customer experience, operations, business model innovation, digital enablers, and organization and people. It helps organizations understand their digital strengths and weaknesses.

KPMG's Digital Transformation Framework

KPMG's Digital Transformation Framework guides organizations through the process of digital transformation, covering strategy, customer experience, operations, and technology. It emphasizes the importance of a customer-centric approach and organizational agility.

IBM's Digital Reinvention

IBM's Digital Reinvention framework focuses on helping organizations reinvent themselves in the digital era. It includes strategies for adopting emerging technologies, enhancing customer experiences, and transforming business models.It's important to note that while these consulting companies provide frameworks and methodologies, the specific strategies implemented by organizations may vary based on their unique needs, industry, and goals. Organizations often tailor these frameworks to align with their specific digital transformation objectives and challenges.

Examples of Methods used by Digital consulting companies

Method 1: Customer-centric approach

Top consulting companies like Accenture, BCG, and Deloitte emphasize the importance of a customer-centric approach to digital transformation. This means understanding customer needs and preferences, and using technology to create a seamless and personalized customer experience across all touchpoints.

Accenture: Accenture uses its Design Thinking methodology to help organizations understand the needs and desires of their customers. They also offer a suite of digital marketing and customer experience management (CXM) solutions to help organizations deliver exceptional customer experiences.

BCG: BCG uses its proprietary customer journey mapping tool to help organizations identify and map out the customer journey across all touchpoints. They also offer a range of services to help organizations improve customer experience, including customer service training, voice of the customer (VOC) programs, and social media listening.

Deloitte: Deloitte uses its Customer Data Platform (CDP) to help organizations collect, analyze, and use customer data to create personalized experiences. They also offer a range of services to help organizations optimize their marketing and sales campaigns, and improve customer loyalty.

Method 2: Data-driven decision-making

Top consulting companies like IBM, Capgemini, and EY recognize the importance of data-driven decision-making in the digital age. This means using data analytics to uncover insights that can inform strategic decisions, improve operational efficiency, and drive innovation.

IBM: IBM offers a wide range of data analytics and artificial intelligence (AI) solutions to help organizations gain insights from their data. They also offer consulting services to help organizations develop data governance frameworks, implement data analytics initiatives, and integrate AI into their business operations.

Capgemini: Capgemini helps organizations implement data-driven decision-making processes across their entire organization. They also offer a range of services to help organizations improve their data quality, and build a culture of data literacy.

EY: EY helps organizations use data to identify and exploit new business opportunities. They also offer services to help organizations improve their data security, and comply with data privacy regulations.

Method 3: Agile and collaborative work environments

Top consulting companies like KPMG and PwC recognize the importance of agile and collaborative work environments for successful digital transformation. This means creating a culture of innovation and experimentation, and fostering collaboration between different teams and departments.

KPMG: KPMG helps organizations develop agile work processes and methodologies to adapt to the changing digital landscape. They also offer services to help organizations improve communication and collaboration between employees, and break down silos between different teams.

PwC: PwC helps organizations create a culture of innovation and experimentation by incorporating design thinking and lean startup principles into their work processes. They also offer services to help organizations foster collaboration between employees from different backgrounds and disciplines.

Method 4: Secure and trusted digital ecosystems

Top consulting companies like Accenture and Deloitte recognize the importance of security in the digital age. They help organizations develop cybersecurity strategies to protect their data and systems from cyberattacks.

Accenture: Accenture offers a range of cybersecurity services to help organizations identify and mitigate cyberthreats. They also help organizations develop incident response plans and improve their overall cybersecurity posture.

Deloitte: Deloitte helps organizations develop a comprehensive approach to cybersecurity that includes risk assessment, vulnerability management, and threat intelligence. They also offer training and awareness programs to help employees protect themselves and the organization from cyberattacks.

Method 5: Future-ready talent and skills

Top consulting companies like McKinsey and Bain recognize the importance of talent in the digital age. They help organizations develop the skills and capabilities required for the digital workforce.

McKinsey: McKinsey helps organizations identify and develop the talent required for the digital age. They also offer services to help organizations design and implement training programs, and foster a culture of continuous learning.

Bain: Bain helps organizations attract and retain top talent in the digital economy. They also offer services to help organizations develop leadership development programs, and create a workplace that is attractive to digital natives.

Digital Leadership

Digital transformation leadership is the process of guiding an organization through the process of transitioning from a traditional, analog business model to a digital, data-driven one. This requires a combination of strategic thinking, technological expertise, and people leadership.

Key responsibilities of digital transformation leaders

Develop a clear vision for digital transformation: Leaders must articulate a compelling vision for how digital transformation can transform the organization and its performance. This vision should be aligned with the organization's overall business strategy and should be communicated effectively to all stakeholders.

Set strategic goals and objectives: Leaders must establish clear goals and objectives for digital transformation initiatives. These goals should be measurable and achievable, and they should be aligned with the organization's overall strategic priorities.

Identify and prioritize digital transformation opportunities: Leaders must identify and prioritize the most promising digital transformation opportunities. This requires a deep understanding of the organization's current business landscape, its competitive landscape, and the latest technological trends.

Select and implement the right technologies: Leaders must select and implement the right technologies to support the organization's digital transformation initiatives. This requires a thorough understanding of the organization's needs and a willingness to experiment with new technologies.

Drive organizational change: Digital transformation requires significant organizational change. Leaders must drive this change by creating a culture of innovation and collaboration, and by empowering employees to embrace new ways of working.

Measure and evaluate progress: Leaders must continuously measure and evaluate the progress of digital transformation initiatives. This requires establishing key performance indicators (KPIs) and collecting data to track progress.

Qualities of effective digital transformation leaders

Visionary: Digital transformation leaders must have a clear vision for how digital transformation can transform the organization. They should be able to articulate this vision effectively to others and inspire people to follow.

Strategic: Digital transformation leaders must be strategic thinkers. They should be able to analyze complex business problems and develop effective solutions.

Technologically savvy: Digital transformation leaders should have a strong understanding of technology trends and how they can be used to improve business processes and customer experiences.

People-focused: Digital transformation leaders must be able to inspire and motivate people to embrace change. They should be able to build trust and collaborate effectively with others.

Resilient: Digital transformation is not without its challenges. Leaders must be able to persevere in the face of setbacks and maintain a positive outlook.

Benefits of effective digital transformation leadership

Improved customer experiences: Digital transformation can lead to improved customer experiences by providing them with more personalized and convenient interactions.

Increased operational efficiency: Digital transformation can lead to increased operational efficiency by automating tasks, streamlining processes, and reducing costs.

Enhanced innovation: Digital transformation can foster innovation by providing access to new technologies and data insights.

Enhanced competitive advantage: Digital transformation can help organizations gain a competitive advantage by enabling them to adapt to market changes faster and more effectively than their competitors.

Stronger market position: Digital transformation can help organizations strengthen their market position by making them more attractive to customers, partners, and investors.

In conclusion, digital transformation leadership is a critical role in today's business world. Leaders who can effectively guide their organizations through the digital transformation process will be well-positioned for success in the years to come.

- Executive Leadership:
- Chief Digital Officer (CDO)
- Chief Information Officer (CIO)
- Chief Technology Officer (CTO)
- Chief Innovation Officer (CIO)
- Chief Security Officer (CISO)
- Strategy and Planning:
- Digital transformation strategist
- Business transformation consultant
- Change management consultant
- Project manager
- Strategic planning manager
- Technology and Architecture:
- Cloud architect
- Data architect
- Infrastructure engineer
- Software developer
- Security engineer
- Customer Experience and Marketing:
- Digital marketing manager
- UX/UI designer
- Product manager
- Customer experience manager
- Marketing automation specialist
- Data and Analytics:
- Data scientist

- Data analyst
- Business intelligence analyst
- Data engineer
- Machine learning engineer
- Human Resources and Communication:
- Human resources manager
- Communication specialist
- Training and development manager
- Change management specialist
- Employee engagement manager
- Business Process Automation (BPA):
- BPA specialist
- Process analyst
- Business process improvement specialist
- Workflow automation specialist
- Robotic process automation (RPA) specialist
- Cybersecurity and Risk Management:
- Cybersecurity specialist
- Risk management specialist
- Security engineer
- Vulnerability assessment specialist
- Security awareness specialist
- Legal and Compliance:
- Legal counsel
- Compliance officer
- Privacy officer
- Data protection officer (DPO)
- Intellectual property (IP) attorney
- Other Relevant Roles:

- Innovation manager
- Agile coach
- Design thinking consultant
- User experience (UX) researcher
- Customer experience (CX) researcher
- Artificial intelligence (AI) specialist
- Machine learning (ML) specialist

CEOs play a crucial role in driving digital transformation within organizations. They are responsible for setting the vision, providing leadership, and allocating resources to ensure that the organization's digital transformation initiatives are successful.

Key aspects of CEO thinking in digital transformation:

Understanding the business case for digital transformation: CEOs need to be able to articulate the compelling reasons why their organization needs to undergo digital transformation. This includes understanding how digital technologies can improve customer experience, increase operational efficiency, and drive innovation.

Setting a clear vision for digital transformation: CEOs need to set a clear vision for what they want their organization to achieve through digital transformation. This vision should be ambitious but achievable, and it should be aligned with the organization's overall business strategy.

Establishing clear goals and objectives: CEOs need to break down the overall vision for digital transformation into clear goals and objectives. These goals and objectives should be measurable and achievable, and they should be communicated to all employees.

Selecting the right technologies: CEOs need to understand the latest and greatest digital technologies, and they need to be able to select the right technologies for their organization's needs. This includes considering factors such as cost, scalability, security, and compatibility with existing systems.

Driving organizational change: Digital transformation requires significant organizational change. CEOs need to create a culture of innovation and collaboration, and they need to empower employees to embrace new ways of working.

Measuring and evaluating progress: CEOs need to continuously measure and evaluate the progress of their organization's digital transformation initiatives. This includes establishing key performance indicators (KPIs) and collecting data to track progress.

In addition to these key aspects, CEOs also need to be mindful of the following challenges:

Legacy systems and infrastructure: Many organizations have legacy systems and infrastructure that may need to be upgraded or replaced in order to support digital transformation initiatives.

Cultural resistance: Some employees may resist change, and CEOs need to be prepared to address this resistance.

The pace of change: The pace of technological change is rapid, and CEOs need to be able to adapt quickly to ensure that their organization remains competitive.

Despite these challenges, CEOs who are able to effectively lead their organizations through digital transformation can reap significant benefits, such as:

Improved customer experience: Digital technologies can be used to create more personalized and convenient customer experiences.

Increased operational efficiency: Digital technologies can automate tasks, streamline processes, and reduce costs.

Enhanced innovation: Digital technologies can foster innovation by providing access to new data and insights.

Enhanced competitive advantage: Digital transformation can help organizations gain a competitive advantage by enabling them to adapt to market changes faster and more effectively than their competitors.

In conclusion, CEO thinking is critical to the success of digital transformation. By understanding the key aspects of CEO thinking, organizations can increase their chances of achieving their digital transformation goals.

Essential traits of effective digital transformation leadership:

Visionary Leadership

The ability to articulate a clear and compelling vision for how digital technologies will transform the organization. A visionary leader can inspire and motivate teams by illustrating the benefits and possibilities of digital transformation.

Adaptability and Agility:

The digital landscape evolves rapidly. Leaders must be adaptable and agile, able to respond to changing technologies, market conditions, and organizational needs. Flexibility is key to navigating uncertainties and seizing new opportunities.

Strategic Thinking:

Strategic leaders can align digital initiatives with overall business goals.

They understand the broader implications of digital transformation and can develop a roadmap that aligns with the organization's long-term strategy.

Change Management Skills

Digital transformation often involves significant organizational change. Leaders need strong change management skills to guide teams through transitions, manage resistance, and foster a culture that embraces continuous improvement.

Collaborative Mindset:

Collaboration is essential in a digital transformation journey. Leaders should be adept at building cross-functional teams, fostering collaboration across departments, and ensuring that diverse stakeholders are aligned and engaged.

Customer-Centric Focus:

Successful digital transformation is often centered around improving the customer experience. Leaders must have a deep understanding of customer needs and behaviors, using this insight to drive digital initiatives that enhance satisfaction and loyalty.

Data-Driven Decision-Making:

Leaders should be comfortable leveraging data analytics to make informed decisions. They understand the importance of data in driving insights, measuring performance, and optimizing processes.

Risk-Taking and Innovation:

Digital transformation involves some level of risk. Leaders need to be comfortable taking calculated risks, fostering a culture of innovation, and encouraging experimentation and learning from failures.

Tech Savvy:

A solid understanding of emerging technologies is crucial. While leaders don't need to be experts in every technology, they should have a foundational knowledge to make informed decisions and effectively communicate with technology teams.

Communication Skills:

Clear and effective communication is vital. Leaders must be able to convey the benefits and goals of digital transformation to all levels of the organization, ensuring understanding and buy-in.

Commitment to Continuous Learning:

The digital landscape is constantly evolving. Leaders should have a commitment to continuous learning, staying informed about new technologies, industry trends, and best practices in digital transformation.

These traits collectively contribute to effective digital transformation leadership, enabling organizations to navigate the complexities of the digital age successfully.

ARISE: Pursuit of Technology

Embark on an enlightening odyssey through the dynamic landscape of 'Arise: Pursuit of Technology,' where we delve into the forefront of technological innovation. Join us as we explore the revolutionary realms of Artificial Intelligence (AI), Machine Learning (ML), Industry X.0 & Robotics, Blockchain, Digital Twins & Robotics, and Augmented/Virtual/Mixed Reality (AR/VR/MR).

In this immersive journey, gain profound insights into the limitless possibilities, intricate challenges, and the transformative impact these cutting-edge technologies wield on the ever-evolving tapestry of business and communication. From the intricate algorithms of AI and ML to the disruptive potential of Industry X.0, from the decentralized power of Blockchain to the symbiotic relationship between Digital Twins and Robotics, and from the captivating experiences of AR/VR/MR to the interconnected future they unveil, 'Arise' promises an exploration of unparalleled depth and breadth.

Dive into the intricate tapestry of each technological frontier, unraveling the threads that weave together opportunities, challenges, and the unprecedented influence these advancements exert on the global landscape. 'Arise: Pursuit of Technology' beckons you to be at the forefront of the technological revolution, where innovation meets insight, and the future unfolds before your eyes.

Data & Cloud

Developing a robust data strategy is a critical component of successful digital transformation initiatives. A well-defined data strategy ensures that organizations can effectively leverage data to drive innovation, enhance decision-making, and achieve their business goals. Here are key elements and considerations for crafting a comprehensive data strategy in the context of digital transformation:

Business Alignment Align data strategy with overall business objectives and digital transformation goals. Understand how data can contribute to achieving strategic objectives, improving operations, and enhancing customer experiences.

Data Ownership and Accountability: Clearly define data ownership and accountability within the organization. Establish governance frameworks to ensure the quality, security, and compliance of data throughout its lifecycle.

Scalable Infrastructure: Design a scalable and flexible data architecture that accommodates current and future needs. Consider cloud-based solutions for scalability, cost-effectiveness, and accessibility.

Data Quality Standards: Implement data quality standards to ensure accuracy, completeness, and consistency. Develop robust data integration processes to facilitate seamless data flow across systems and platforms.

Security Measures: Implement robust data security measures to protect sensitive information. Ensure compliance with relevant data protection regulations and industry standards.

End-to-End Management: Define a comprehensive data lifecycle management strategy, covering data acquisition, storage, processing, analysis, and archival. This includes data retention policies and archival procedures.

Advanced Analytics: Define strategies for implementing advanced analytics, including machine learning and artificial intelligence, to derive actionable insights from data. Enable data-driven decision-making at all levels of the organization.

Cultural Shift: Foster a data-driven culture within the organization. Promote the importance of data literacy and provide training to ensure employees have the necessary skills to work with data effectively.

Ethical Use of Data: Establish guidelines for the ethical use of data, ensuring that privacy considerations are taken into account. Communicate transparently about how customer data is collected, stored, and used.

External Data Sources: Consider how to leverage external data sources and collaborate with partners to enrich internal datasets. Explore opportunities to create a data ecosystem that enhances business intelligence.

KPIs and Metrics: Define key performance indicators (KPIs) and metrics to measure the success of the data strategy. Regularly assess the impact of data initiatives on business outcomes.

Iterative Improvement: Adopt an agile approach to data strategy, allowing for continuous improvement and adaptation based on evolving business needs and technological advancements.

Monetization Opportunities: Explore opportunities for monetizing data, whether through new product offerings, partnerships, or data-driven insights that can be valuable to external entities.

Risk Assessment: Conduct a thorough risk assessment to identify potential risks associated with data, including security breaches, compliance issues, and reputational risks. Develop mitigation strategies accordingly.

A well-crafted data strategy serves as a roadmap for organizations seeking to capitalize on the transformative power of data. It aligns data initiatives with business objectives, ensures data quality and security, fosters a data-driven culture, and supports the overall success of digital transformation efforts. Regularly revisit and update the data strategy to stay aligned with changing business needs and technological advancements.

Cloud Strategy in a Digital Transformation

A cloud strategy is a crucial component of a successful digital transformation initiative, as it outlines how an organization will leverage cloud computing to achieve its business goals. A well-defined cloud strategy helps organizations optimize costs, improve agility, and gain access to a vast array of cloud-based services and technologies.

Key Elements of a Cloud Strategy for Digital Transformation

A comprehensive cloud strategy for digital transformation encompasses the following key elements:

Cloud adoption strategy: Define the scope of cloud adoption, including the types of workloads, applications, and data that will be migrated to the cloud.

Cloud service model: Select the appropriate cloud service model, such as

Infrastructure as a Service (IaaS), Platform as a Service (PaaS), or Software as a Service (SaaS), based on business needs and requirements.

Cloud provider selection: Evaluate and select the most suitable cloud provider, considering factors such as scalability, performance, security, and cost.

Cloud migration strategy: Develop a detailed plan for migrating applications and data to the cloud, ensuring data integrity, minimal downtime, and smooth integration with existing systems.

Cloud cost optimization: Implement strategies to optimize cloud costs, including resource allocation, cloud governance, and cost management tools.

Cloud security: Establish robust security measures to protect cloud-based assets, data, and applications from unauthorized access, cyberattacks, and data breaches.

Cloud governance: Define clear policies and procedures to govern cloud usage, ensure compliance with regulations, and maintain control over cloud infrastructure and applications.

Benefits of a Cloud Strategy for Digital Transformation

Adopting a cloud strategy can bring numerous benefits to organizations undergoing digital transformation:

Cost optimization: Cloud computing can help organizations reduce IT infrastructure costs by eliminating the need for on-premises hardware, software, and maintenance expenses.

Agility and scalability: Cloud-based systems offer greater flexibility and scalability, enabling organizations to quickly adapt to changing business needs and market demands.

Access to innovation: Cloud providers offer access to a vast array of innovative cloud-based services and technologies, empowering organizations to explore new opportunities and enhance their digital capabilities.

Enhanced collaboration and productivity: Cloud-based tools and applications facilitate collaboration and communication across teams, improving productivity and efficiency.

Data agility and analytics: Cloud-based data management and analytics tools allow organizations to gather, analyze, and utilize data more effectively, gaining valuable insights for decision-making.

Global reach and accessibility: Cloud-based services can be accessed from anywhere with an internet connection, enabling organizations to expand their reach and support a global workforce.

A cloud strategy serves as a roadmap for organizations to harness the power of cloud computing and accelerate their digital transformation journey. By prioritizing cloud adoption, optimizing costs, and leveraging cloud-based capabilities, organizations can gain a competitive advantage in the digital era.

Artificial Intelligent

Artificial intelligence (AI) plays a transformative role in digital transformation initiatives, enabling organizations to enhance their operations, optimize decision-making, and gain a competitive edge. AI-powered technologies are revolutionizing various industries, driving innovation and efficiency across the entire value chain.

AI Circle of explanation

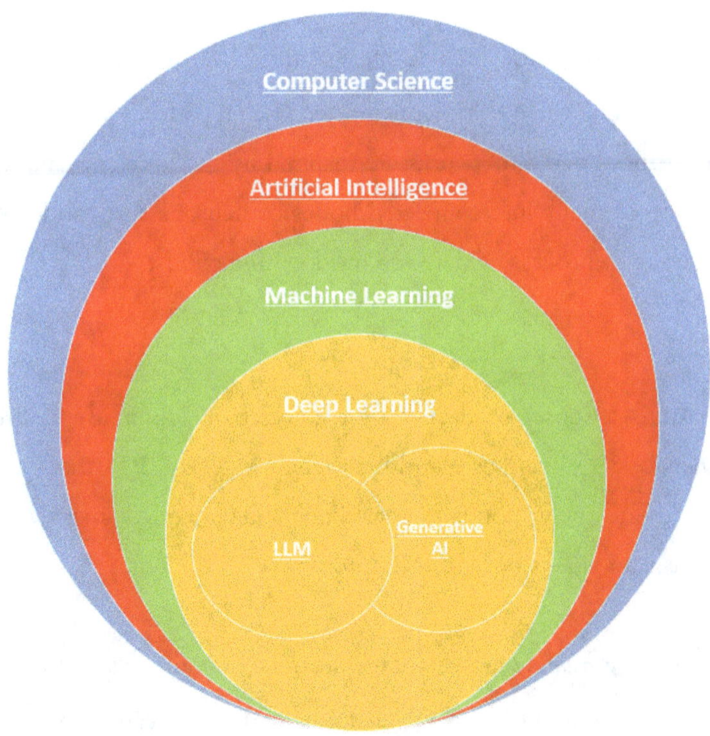

AI Circle of explanation

AI is a branch of computer science that deals with the creation of intelligence agents, which are systems that can reason, and learn, and act autonomously.Science that empowers computers to mimic human intelligence such as decision making, text processing, and visual perception

Machine learning which is a subfield of AI gives the computer the ability to learn without explicit programming.ML is the science of developing algorithms and statistical models that computer systems use to perform complex tasks without explicit instructions.

Deep learning is a type of machine learning that uses artificial neural networks, allowing them to process more complex patterns than machine learning.Artificial neural networks are inspired by the human brain. They are made up of many interconnected nodes or neurons that can learn to perform tasks by processing data and making predictions.

Gen AI

Gen AI is a subset of deep learning, which means it uses artificial neural networks, describes algorithms (such as ChatGPT) that can be used to create new content, including audio, code, images, text, simulations, and videos by input NL/prompt

Large language models are very large deep learning models that are pre-trained on vast amounts of data. that can perform a variety of natural language processing (NLP) tasks such as generating and classifying text, answering questions in a conversational manner, and translating text from one language to another

A foundation model is a large AI model pre-trained on a vast quantity of data designed to be adapted
or fine tuned to a wide range of downstream tasks, such as sentiment analysis, image captioning, and object recognition.

Generative AI and Large Language Models (LLMs)

Generative AI is a type of artificial intelligence that focuses on creating new content, such as text, images, music, and code. It uses machine learning algorithms to learn from existing data and then generate new output that is similar to the data it has seen.

Large language models (LLMs) are a type of generative AI that is trained on a massive amount of text data. This allows them to generate human-quality text, translate languages, write different kinds of creative content, and answer your questions in an informative way.

Key Features of Generative AI and LLMs

Creativity: Generative AI can create new content that is original and engaging. LLMs can generate creative text formats, like poems, code, scripts, musical pieces, email, letters, etc.

Adaptability: Generative AI can adapt to different kinds of data and tasks. LLMs can be fine-tuned to specific domains or tasks, such as generating product descriptions, writing marketing copy, or summarizing scientific papers.

Open-endedness: Generative AI can generate new content that is not explicitly programmed. LLMs can generate new text formats, translate languages, write different kinds of creative content, and answer your questions in an informative way.

Applications of Generative AI and LLMs

Content creation: Generative AI can be used to create new content, such as blog posts, articles, scripts, and musical pieces.

Translation: LLMs can translate languages with high accuracy.

Customer service: LLMs can be used to provide customer service chatbots that can answer questions and resolve issues.

Education: LLMs can be used to create personalized learning experiences and provide feedback to students.

Research: LLMs can be used to analyze data, generate hypotheses, and create new theories.

Bias: Generative AI can reflect and amplify existing biases in the data it is trained on.

Misinformation: LLMs can be used to generate fake news and misinformation.

Explainability: It can be difficult to understand how generative AI makes decisions, which can make it difficult to trust its outputs.

Ethics: There are ethical concerns about the use of generative AI, such as its potential to be misused for harmful purposes.

Future of Generative AI and LLMs

Generative AI and LLMs have the potential to revolutionize many industries, from content creation to customer service to education. As these technologies continue to develop, we can expect to see even more innovative and transformative applications emerge.

The field of generative artificial intelligence (AI) and large language models (LLMs) is rapidly evolving, with new players emerging all the time. Here are some of the major players in this field:

Google AI: Google AI is one of the leading developers of generative AI and LLMs. Their flagship LLM, LaMDA, has been shown to be capable of generating human-quality text, translating languages, and answering questions in an informative way.

OpenAI: OpenAI is a non-profit research company that focuses on developing safe and beneficial AI. Their LLM, GPT-3, is one of the most powerful LLMs in the world.

Microsoft: Microsoft is also developing LLMs, with their flagship model, Turing, being particularly focused on dialogue and question answering.

Meta AI (formerly Facebook AI Research): Meta AI is the research division of Meta (formerly Facebook), and they are developing some of the most advanced LLMs in the world, including Jurassic-1 Jumbo.

Baidu: Baidu is a Chinese tech giant that is also developing LLMs, with their flagship model, ERNIE 3.0, being particularly focused on natural language understanding.

Hugging Face: Hugging Face is a company that provides open-source tools for developing and deploying LLMs. Their model zoo is a popular resource for LLM researchers and developers.

EleutherAI: EleutherAI is a non-profit research organization that develops and releases open-source LLMs. They are known for their work on large, high-quality language models, such as Megatron-Turing NLG 530B.

This is just a small sample of the many players in the field of generative AI and LLMs. As these technologies continue to develop, we can expect to see even more innovation and competition in the years to come.

Google AI is committed to developing generative AI (Gen AI) and large language models (LLMs) that are safe, reliable, and beneficial to society. We believe that these technologies have the potential to revolutionize many industries, from content creation to customer service to education.

Here are some of the ways Google AI is working to advance Gen AI and LLMs:

Developing new models: We are constantly developing new and more powerful Gen AI models, such as LaMDA and PaLM. These models are trained on massive amounts of data, and they are able to generate human-quality text, translate languages, write different kinds of creative content, and answer your questions in an informative way.

Improving explainability: We are working on ways to make Gen AI models more explainable, so that we can better understand how they make decisions. This will help us to identify and address potential biases and errors in the models.

Addressing ethical concerns: We are committed to developing Gen AI and LLMs in a way that is ethical and responsible. We are working with experts from a variety of fields, including computer science, philosophy, and law, to develop guidelines for the responsible use of these technologies.

Enhancing safety: We are developing new safety mechanisms to prevent Gen AI models from being used for harmful purposes. For example, we are working on ways to detect and prevent the spread of misinformation and hate speech.

Collaborating with the broader AI community: We are collaborating with other AI researchers and companies to advance the field of Gen AI and LLMs. We are sharing our research findings and tools, and we are working together to address common challenges.

Ethics and Responsible AI

Artificial intelligence (AI) is rapidly evolving and becoming increasingly integrated into our lives. As AI becomes more powerful, it is important to consider the ethical implications of its development and use.

Key Ethical Concerns

There are a number of key ethical concerns that need to be addressed in the development and use of AI, including:

Bias: AI can reflect and amplify existing biases in the data it is trained on. This can lead to unfair or discriminatory outcomes.

Privacy: AI systems can collect and store a lot of personal data, which raises privacy concerns.

Transparency: It can be difficult to understand how AI systems make decisions, which can make it difficult to trust their outputs.

Accountability: Who is responsible for the actions of AI systems?

Safety: AI systems can malfunction or be hacked, which could have serious consequences.

Responsible AI Development

To address these ethical concerns, we need to develop and use AI in a responsible manner. This includes:

- Being aware of the potential biases in our data and taking steps to mitigate them.
- Protecting the privacy of users.
- Ensuring that AI systems are transparent and explainable.
- Developing mechanisms for accountability.
- Taking steps to ensure the safety of AI systems.
- Guiding Principles for Responsible AI

There are a number of guiding principles that can help us to develop and use AI in a responsible manner, including:

Human oversight: Human decision-makers should always be in control of AI systems.

Human benefit: AI should be developed and used to benefit humanity.

Safety and security: AI systems should be safe and secure.

Fairness and non-discrimination: AI systems should not discriminate against individuals or groups.

Explainability: AI systems should be explainable.

Accountability: There should be clear accountability for the development and use of AI systems.

Collaboration and Openness

It is important to collaborate with experts from a variety of fields, including computer science, philosophy, and law, to develop guidelines for the responsible use of AI. We also need to be open and transparent about the development and use of AI systems so that we can identify and address potential problems.

Key Applications of AI in Digital Transformation

AI is being applied in diverse areas to drive digital transformation, including:

Product development: AI-powered tools assist in product design, testing, and optimization, leading to innovative and high-quality products.

Customer experience: AI-driven personalization and recommendation engines enhance customer interactions, fostering loyalty and satisfaction.

Operations optimization: AI-based predictive analytics identify potential issues and optimize resource allocation, improving efficiency and reducing costs.

Risk management: AI-powered fraud detection and cybersecurity solutions safeguard organizations from financial losses and reputational damage.

Human resources: AI-driven recruitment platforms and performance management systems enhance HR processes, attracting top talent and maximizing employee engagement.

Supply chain management: AI-powered logistics optimization, inventory management, and predictive maintenance drive efficiency and cost savings throughout the supply chain.

Marketing and sales: AI-based customer segmentation, personalized marketing campaigns, and chatbots enhance customer engagement and drive sales.

Fraud detection and prevention: AI-powered tools analyze transaction patterns and data to identify and prevent fraudulent activities.

Risk assessment and modeling: AI-based tools analyze data to assess risks, optimize insurance premiums, and inform investment decisions.

Content creation and personalization: AI-powered tools generate creative content, personalize news feeds, and provide tailored recommendations.

Robotics and automation: AI-driven robots automate repetitive tasks, enhancing efficiency and safety.

Benefits of AI in Digital Transformation

Adopting AI in digital transformation initiatives brings numerous benefits:

Enhanced productivity: AI-powered automation and optimization tools free up human resources to focus on more strategic and creative tasks.

Improved decision-making: AI-driven insights and predictive analytics enable organizations to make informed decisions based on real-time data and trends.

Reduced costs: AI-based automation and optimization can lead to cost savings across various operations.

Enhanced customer experience: personalized and tailored experiences foster customer satisfaction and loyalty.

Accelerated innovation: AI-powered tools accelerate product development, marketing campaigns, and process improvements.

Reduced risks and fraud: AI-driven risk assessment and detection tools protect organizations from financial losses and reputational damage.

Conclusion

AI is a powerful tool that has the potential to benefit society in many ways. However, it is important to use AI responsibly and ethically. By following the guiding principles outlined above, we can ensure that AI is developed and used in a way that benefits all of humanity.

Organizations need to view AI and Gen AI as transformative technologies that have the potential to revolutionize their businesses and industries. To fully harness the potential of AI and Gen AI, organizations need to adopt a strategic approach that encompasses the following key aspects:

Cultivate a culture of innovation and experimentation: Organizations need to foster a culture that encourages experimentation and risk-taking, as this is essential for exploring the full potential of AI and Gen AI. This includes providing employees with the resources and support they need to develop new AI-powered solutions and initiatives.

Invest in AI talent and expertise: Organizations need to invest in building a team of AI talent, including data scientists, engineers, and machine learning experts. This talent will be responsible for developing, deploying, and maintaining AI and Gen AI solutions throughout the organization.

Establish clear AI and Gen AI goals and objectives: Organizations need to clearly define their AI and Gen AI goals and objectives. These goals should align with the organization's overall business strategy and should be measurable and achievable.

Develop a comprehensive AI and Gen AI roadmap: Organizations need to develop a comprehensive AI and Gen AI roadmap that outlines the steps they will take to achieve their goals. This roadmap should include a plan for identifying and prioritizing AI projects, as well as a plan for managing and governing AI usage within the organization.

Implement robust data governance and security measures: Organizations need to implement robust data governance and security measures to protect the privacy and integrity of their data. This includes ensuring that data is collected, stored, and used in a responsible manner, and that it is protected from unauthorized access and breaches.

Partner with external AI experts: Organizations may need to partner with external AI experts to help them develop, deploy, and manage AI and Gen AI solutions. These experts can provide valuable insights and expertise that can help organizations navigate the complex world of AI.

Continuously monitor and evaluate AI and Gen AI performance: Organizations need to continuously monitor and evaluate the performance of their AI and Gen AI solutions. This will help them identify areas where improvements can be made and ensure that their AI solutions are meeting their intended goals.

Ensure AI and Gen AI are aligned with ethical principles: Organizations need to ensure that their AI and Gen AI solutions are aligned with ethical principles. This includes ensuring that AI is used in a fair, unbiased, and non-discriminatory manner.

Industry x.0

The History of Industry 4.0

The term "Industry 4.0" was coined in 2011 by a group of experts at the Hannover Messe, a trade fair for industrial technology in Germany. The concept was further developed by the German government, which released a strategy paper in 2013 outlining the goals and opportunities of Industry 4.0.

Industry 4.0 builds on the foundations of the previous three industrial revolutions:

Industry 1.0 (1760-1840): The first industrial revolution was characterized by the mechanization of production, with the introduction of steam power and water power.

Industry 2.0 (1870-1914): The second industrial revolution was characterized by the mass production of goods, with the introduction of assembly lines and standardized parts.

Industry 3.0 (1970-present): The third industrial revolution was characterized by the digitization of production, with the introduction of computers and automation.

Industry 4.0 is characterized by the convergence of several technologies, including:

- Artificial intelligence (AI): AI is used to automate tasks, improve decision-making, and personalize products and services.

- Augmented reality (AR): AR is used to overlay digital information onto the real world, providing workers with real-time guidance and instructions.

- Robotics: Robots are used to automate tasks, improve safety, and increase productivity.

- Internet of Things (IoT): IoT is used to connect physical devices to the internet, enabling real-time monitoring and data collection.

- Cyber-physical systems (CPS): CPS are systems that combine physical and digital components, enabling the real-time monitoring and control of physical systems.

Industry 4.0 is transforming the way businesses operate across a wide range of industries, including manufacturing, healthcare, retail, transportation, and energy.

Examples of how Industry 4.0 is being used:

- In manufacturing,: robots are being used to automate tasks, such as welding, painting, and assembly. AI is being used to optimize production schedules and predict equipment failures. IoT is being used to monitor the performance of machinery and equipment.

- In healthcare,: AI is being used to diagnose diseases, provide personalized treatment plans, and develop new drugs. AR is being used to guide surgeons during operations and provide real-time feedback. IoT is being used to monitor patients' health data and track their progress.

- In retail,: AI is being used to recommend products to customers, personalize online shopping experiences, and optimize inventory management. AR is being used to help customers visualize products in their homes before they buy them. IoT is being used to track the movement of products through the supply chain.

- In transportation,: autonomous vehicles are being developed to navigate roads without human intervention. AI is being used to optimize traffic flow and reduce congestion. IoT is being used to monitor the performance of vehicles and track their location.

- In energy,: smart grids are being developed to collect and analyze data from energy sources and consumers. AI is being used to optimize energy production and distribution. IoT is being used to monitor the performance of energy infrastructure and identify potential problems.

Industry 4.0 is a rapidly evolving field, and new technologies are emerging all the time. As these technologies mature, they will continue to transform the way businesses operate and industries interact.

Industry 4.0, often referred to as the fourth industrial revolution, is a transformative approach to manufacturing and industry that leverages advanced technologies to create smart, connected, and automated systems. It involves the integration of digital technologies, the Internet of Things (IoT), artificial intelligence (AI), cloud computing, and data analytics to optimize industrial processes. Here are details about Industry 4.0 and how it is implemented in manufacturing sites:

Industry 4.0 in Manufacturing Sites:

Smart Factories:

Connected Machinery: Installing sensors on production equipment to monitor performance and gather data.

Networked Systems: Creating a network of interconnected machines and systems for seamless communication and collaboration.

Predictive Maintenance:

Condition Monitoring: Implementing IoT sensors to monitor the condition of machinery in real-time.

Predictive Analytics: Using data analytics and AI to predict when equipment is likely to fail, allowing for proactive maintenance.

Digital Twin Technology:

Virtual Prototyping: Developing digital twins of physical assets *to simulate and test production processes virtually.*

Real-Time Monitoring: Using digital twins to monitor and analyze the performance of physical assets in real-time.

Supply Chain Integration:

Smart Logistics: Incorporating IoT devices to track and trace materials throughout the supply chain.

Demand Sensing: Using data analytics to predict demand patterns and optimize inventory levels.

Quality Control and Assurance:

Automated Inspection: Implementing automated inspection systems using computer vision and AI.

Real-Time Feedback: Providing real-time feedback on production quality to enable immediate corrective actions.

Agile Manufacturing:

Flexible Production Lines: Designing production lines that can be easily reconfigured to adapt to changing product requirements.

Batch Size One: Implementing production capabilities that allow for customized, on-demand manufacturing.

Employee Empowerment:

Training with Augmented Reality (AR): Using AR technologies to provide training and guidance to workers.

Human-Machine Collaboration: Encouraging collaboration between human workers and intelligent machines to enhance productivity.

Energy Efficiency:

Energy Monitoring: Utilizing IoT sensors to monitor energy consumption across the manufacturing site.

Optimized Operations: Using data analytics to identify opportunities for energy efficiency and sustainability.

Continuous Improvement:

Data-Driven Decision-Making: Empowering decision-makers with real-time data and insights for continuous improvement.

Iterative Implementation: Embracing an iterative approach to technology adoption, allowing for ongoing adjustments and enhancements.

Security and Data Privacy:

Cybersecurity Measures: Implementing robust cybersecurity measures to protect sensitive industrial data.

Data Encryption: Ensuring that data transmitted between devices and systems is encrypted to prevent unauthorized access.

Regulatory Compliance:

Compliance Monitoring: Implementing systems to monitor and ensure compliance with industry regulations and standards.

Traceability: Utilizing digital systems to provide traceability of products and processes for regulatory purposes.

The implementation of Industry 4.0 concepts in manufacturing sites is a holistic and gradual process that involves the integration of various technologies. It requires strategic planning, investment in digital infrastructure, and a cultural shift towards embracing innovation and digital transformation. The goal is to create more agile, efficient, and adaptive manufacturing processes that can respond to dynamic market demands and technological advancements.

Industry 4.0 is implemented through a number of key steps:

Identifying opportunities: Businesses need to identify the opportunities where Industry 4.0 can be applied to their operations. This may involve reviewing current processes, identifying areas for improvement, and exploring new technologies.

Developing a strategy: Once opportunities have been identified, businesses need to develop a strategy for implementing Industry 4.0. This strategy should outline the goals, objectives, and timeline for the implementation project.

Selecting technologies: Businesses need to select the appropriate technologies for their Industry 4.0 implementation. This may involve considering factors such as cost, scalability, and integration with existing systems.

Implementing technologies: Businesses need to implement the selected technologies in a phased approach. This will allow for testing, learning, and adaptation as the project progresses.

Training and upskilling: Businesses need to train their employees on the new technologies and processes that are being implemented. This will ensure that they are able to use the technologies effectively and efficiently.

Benefits of Industry 4.0

Industry 4.0 can offer a number of benefits to businesses, including:

Increased productivity and efficiency: Industry 4.0 can automate tasks, optimize processes, and provide real-time data insights, which can lead to increased productivity and efficiency.

New business models: Industry 4.0 can enable the creation of new business models, such as the sharing economy and the Internet of Things.

Personalized customer experiences: Industry 4.0 can provide personalized customer experiences, leading to increased customer satisfaction and loyalty.

Competitive advantage: Businesses that successfully implement Industry 4.0 will gain a competitive advantage over their rivals.

Challenges of Industry 4.0

Industry 4.0 also presents a number of challenges for businesses, including:

Skills gap: There is a shortage of workers with the skills required to implement Industry 4.0 technologies.

Security: Industry 4.0 systems are interconnected and collect vast amounts of data, making them vulnerable to cyberattacks.

Regulation: As Industry 4.0 technologies evolve, new regulations will need to be developed to address ethical, social, and environmental concerns.

Despite these challenges, Industry 4.0 is a powerful tool that can help businesses to achieve their strategic goals. Businesses that are prepared to embrace Industry 4.0 will be well-positioned for success in the years to come.

Digital transformation and Industry 4.0

Digital transformation and Industry 4.0 are two powerful forces that are revolutionizing the way businesses operate. Digital transformation is the process of using digital technologies to improve business processes and customer experiences. Industry 4.0, also known as the fourth industrial revolution, is the convergence of physical and digital technologies to create smart interconnected systems.

Digital transformation and Industry 4.0 are complementary and mutually reinforcing trends. Digital transformation provides the tools and infrastructure that are needed to implement Industry 4.0 technologies. Industry 4.0, in turn, can provide new business opportunities and improve the efficiency and effectiveness of digital transformation initiatives.

Together, digital transformation and Industry 4.0 are creating a new world of possibilities for businesses. Businesses that are able to harness these technologies will be able to gain a competitive advantage and create new value for their customers.

key trends that are shaping the future of digital transformation and Industry 4.0:

The convergence of technologies: The boundaries between different technologies are blurring, creating new and powerful combinations. For example, AI is being used to power IoT devices, and robotics is being used to automate tasks in the cloud.

The rise of the data-driven enterprise: Businesses are collecting and analyzing more data than ever before. This data can be used to gain insights into customer behavior, improve operational efficiency, and develop new products and services.

The automation of tasks: Robots, AI, and other technologies are automating many tasks that were once done by humans. This is leading to increased productivity and efficiency, but it also raises concerns about job displacement.

The personalization of experiences: Businesses are using data and AI to personalize the experiences that they offer to their customers. This can lead to increased customer satisfaction and loyalty.

The creation of new business models: Digital transformation and Industry 4.0 are enabling the creation of new business models that were not possible before. For example, the sharing economy is based on the sharing of resources rather than ownership.

The future of digital transformation and Industry 4.0 is bright. These technologies have the potential to revolutionize the way we live, work, and do business. Businesses that are able to embrace these changes will be well-positioned for success in the years to come.

Siemens: Siemens is a global leader in industrial automation and software, and is working on a number of Industry 4.0 initiatives, including its MindSphere platform, which is a cloud-based IoT platform that connects industrial devices and assets.

General Electric (GE): GE is another global leader in industrial automation, and is working on a number of Industry 4.0 initiatives, including its Predix platform, which is a software platform that collects and analyzes data from industrial equipment.

Rockwell Automation: Rockwell Automation is a leading provider of industrial automation solutions, and is working on a number of Industry 4.0 initiatives, including its FactoryTalk VantagePoint platform, which is a software platform that helps businesses collect, analyze, and visualize data from their industrial operations.

ABB: ABB is a global leader in power and automation technologies, and is working on a number of Industry 4.0 initiatives, including its ABB Ability platform, which is a digital ecosystem that connects ABB's products, services, and software.

Honeywell: Honeywell is a global leader in aerospace, automation and control, and security and fire protection solutions, and is working on a number of Industry 4.0 initiatives, including its Connected Enterprise Platform, which is a cloud-based platform that connects Honeywell's products and services.

PTC: PTC is a leader in product lifecycle management (PLM) software, and is working on a number of Industry 4.0 initiatives, including its ThingWorx platform, which is a platform for developing IoT applications that can include Industry 4.0 capabilities.

Dassault Systèmes: Dassault Systèmes is a leader in 3D design software, and is working on a number of Industry 4.0 initiatives, including its 3DEXPERIENCE platform, which is a cloud-based platform that includes Industry 4.0 capabilities.

Amazon Web Services (AWS): AWS is a leading cloud computing platform, and is working on a number of Industry 4.0 initiatives, including its Amazon Web Services IoT Greengrass service, which is a software platform that allows businesses to deploy and manage IoT devices and applications.

Microsoft Azure: Microsoft Azure is a leading cloud computing platform, and is working on a number of Industry 4.0 initiatives, including its Azure IoT Suite, which is a suite of services for developing and managing IoT applications.

Google Cloud Platform (GCP): GCP is a leading cloud computing platform, and is working on a number of Industry 4.0 initiatives, including its IoT Core service, which is a fully managed service that helps businesses connect and manage IoT devices and data.

These are just a few of the many companies that are working on Industry 4.0. Industry 4.0 is a rapidly growing field, and we can expect to see even more innovation in the coming years.

Blockchain

Blockchain History:

Blockchain, the underlying technology of cryptocurrencies like Bitcoin, has a fascinating history that goes beyond its initial application in digital currencies. Here's an overview of key milestones:

Pre-Bitcoin Era:

1991: Stuart Haber and W. Scott Stornetta proposed a cryptographically secure chain of blocks to timestamp digital documents, preventing backdating or tampering.

Bitcoin Emergence:

2008: An individual or group under the pseudonym Satoshi Nakamoto introduced Bitcoin and its underlying blockchain as a decentralized, peer-to-peer electronic cash system.

Bitcoin Blockchain:

2009: The Bitcoin blockchain went live with the mining of the first block, known as the "genesis block" or Block 0.

Expanding Beyond Bitcoin:

2013: Ethereum was proposed by Vitalik Buterin, introducing the concept of smart contracts and a more generalized blockchain platform.

Rise of ICOs:

2017: Initial Coin Offerings (ICOs) became popular, allowing projects to raise funds through the issuance of new cryptocurrencies.

Enterprise Adoption:

2015-2018: Enterprises began exploring and adopting blockchain for various use cases, leading to the development of permissioned or private blockchains.

Consortium Blockchains:

2015: R3 Corda and Hyperledger projects were initiated, focusing on developing blockchain solutions for consortiums and enterprises.

Blockchain Evolution:

2019-2020: Continued evolution of blockchain technology, with advancements in scalability, interoperability, and the emergence of decentralized finance (DeFi) platforms.

How Blockchain Works:

Blockchain is a decentralized, distributed ledger that records transactions across a network of computers. Here's a simplified explanation of how it works:

Decentralization:

Instead of a central authority, a network of nodes (computers) maintains the blockchain. Each node has a copy of the entire ledger.

Blocks and Transactions:

Transactions are grouped into blocks, and each block contains a reference to the previous block, creating a chain of blocks.

Consensus Mechanism:

Nodes on the network use a consensus mechanism (e.g., Proof of Work in Bitcoin, Proof of Stake in Ethereum) to agree on the validity of transactions and add new blocks.

Cryptography:

Cryptographic techniques secure transactions, ensuring the integrity and immutability of the data. Each block contains a unique identifier (hash), and changing a block requires altering subsequent blocks, making tampering practically impossible.

Smart Contracts (Optional):

In platforms like Ethereum, smart contracts are self-executing contracts with the terms of the agreement directly written into code. They automate processes without the need for intermediaries.

How to Use Blockchain:

Cryptocurrencies:

Transacting in Cryptocurrencies: Use blockchain to send, receive, and store cryptocurrencies like Bitcoin, Ethereum, or other digital assets.

Smart Contracts:

Automated Agreements: Utilize platforms like Ethereum to create and execute smart contracts for automated, trustless agreements.

Supply Chain Management:

Traceability and Transparency: Implement blockchain for supply chain management to track the origin, movement, and authenticity of products.

Identity Management:

Secure Identity Solutions: Develop secure identity management systems using blockchain for authentication and authorization without a central authority.

Voting Systems:

Transparent Voting: Enhance the transparency and security of voting systems by recording votes on a blockchain, minimizing fraud and ensuring integrity.

Cross-Border Payments:

Efficient Cross-Border Transactions: Facilitate faster and more cost-effective cross-border payments using blockchain technology.

Tokenization:

Digital Assets and Tokenization: Tokenize real-world assets, representing ownership or shares, and trade them on blockchain platforms.

Healthcare Records:

Secure Health Data Sharing: Improve the security and interoperability of healthcare records by storing them on a blockchain, controlled by the patient.

Decentralized Finance (DeFi):

Financial Services: Engage in decentralized financial activities, including lending, borrowing, and trading, on DeFi platforms built on blockchain.

Gaming and NFTs:

Non-Fungible Tokens (NFTs): Create and trade unique digital assets, such as in-game items or digital art, using NFTs on blockchain platforms.

Energy Trading:

Peer-to-Peer Energy Trading: Facilitate direct, peer-to-peer energy trading between consumers using blockchain for transparency and efficiency.

Legal and Smart Contracts:

Automated Legal Processes: Utilize smart contracts for automating legal processes, ensuring transparency and efficiency in contract execution.

Real Estate Transactions:

Efficient Property Transactions: Streamline real estate transactions, reducing paperwork and increasing transparency through blockchain.

Intellectual Property Protection:

Timestamping and Proof of Ownership: Use blockchain to timestamp creative works, providing proof of ownership and aiding in intellectual property protection.

Education Credentials:

Secure Credential Verification: Store and verify education credentials securely on a blockchain, allowing for instant and tamper-proof verification.

It's important to note that while blockchain offers various benefits, including transparency, security, and efficiency, it also poses challenges such as scalability, regulatory uncertainties, and energy consumption (in the case of proof-of-work consensus mechanisms). As the technology continues to evolve, its applications and implementations are expected to diversify and mature, providing innovative solutions across industries.

---

key steps and considerations for successfully integrating blockchain technology into an enterprise:

Define Clear Objectives:

Clearly articulate the business objectives and challenges that blockchain aims to address.

Identify specific use cases where blockchain can add value, such as supply chain transparency, smart contracts, or decentralized identity.

Conduct a Feasibility Study:

Assess the feasibility of blockchain implementation by evaluating technical, operational, and regulatory aspects.

Identify potential risks, benefits, and limitations associated with the chosen use cases.

Choose the Right Blockchain Platform:

Select a suitable blockchain platform based on the enterprise's requirements (public, private, or hybrid).

Consider factors like scalability, security, consensus mechanisms, and the level of decentralization needed.

Design the Architecture:

Define the blockchain architecture, including network structure, consensus mechanisms, and data storage.

Determine whether a permissioned or permissionless blockchain is more appropriate based on security and privacy requirements.

Integration with Existing Systems:

Ensure seamless integration with existing enterprise systems (ERP, CRM, etc.).

Develop APIs and middleware solutions for data exchange between blockchain and legacy systems.

Security and Privacy Measures:

Implement robust security measures, including encryption, access controls, and identity management.

Consider privacy-enhancing technologies, especially if dealing with sensitive or private data.

Smart Contracts Development:

Develop smart contracts that automate and enforce business rules.

Ensure the smart contracts align with legal and regulatory requirements.

Selecting Consensus Mechanism:

Choose an appropriate consensus mechanism based on the specific use case and network requirements.

Common mechanisms include Proof of Work (PoW), Proof of Stake (PoS), and Practical Byzantine Fault Tolerance (PBFT).

Governance Model:

Establish a governance model that defines roles, responsibilities, and decision-making processes for participants in the blockchain network.

Ensure compliance with relevant regulations and industry standards.

Pilot Testing:

Conduct pilot testing of the blockchain solution with a small-scale implementation.

Gather feedback from stakeholders and make necessary adjustments based on the pilot results.

Scalability Planning:

Plan for scalability to accommodate the growth of the blockchain network.

Consider solutions such as sharding, layer 2 scaling, or sidechains based on the chosen blockchain platform.

Compliance and Regulations:

Ensure compliance with regulatory requirements relevant to the industry and geographical location.

Work closely with legal experts to navigate regulatory challenges associated with blockchain.

Education and Training:

Provide training for employees involved in blockchain implementation, ensuring they understand the technology and its implications.

Foster a culture of blockchain literacy within the organization.

Collaboration with Partners:

Collaborate with industry partners and stakeholders to establish interoperability standards and promote network effects.

Consider forming or joining industry consortia to share best practices.

Continuous Monitoring and Improvement:

Implement monitoring tools to track the performance, security, and efficiency of the blockchain network.

Iterate and improve the solution based on ongoing feedback and technological advancements.

Documentation and Knowledge Sharing:

Document the entire blockchain implementation process for future reference.

Share knowledge within the organization to build expertise and facilitate continuous improvement.

Community Engagement:

Engage with the blockchain community, attend conferences, and participate in forums to stay informed about industry trends and best practices.

Adoption Plan:

Develop a comprehensive plan for the adoption of blockchain technology across the organization.

Communicate the benefits of blockchain to stakeholders and encourage participation.

Measuring Success:

Establish key performance indicators (KPIs) to measure the success and impact of the blockchain implementation.

Use metrics to assess efficiency gains, cost savings, and improvements in business processes.

Legal and Contractual Considerations:

Ensure that legal contracts and agreements are updated to reflect the use of blockchain technology.

Clarify legal responsibilities and liabilities associated with blockchain transactions.

Technology Partnerships:

Explore partnerships with blockchain solution providers, technology vendors, and industry experts to leverage their expertise and support.

Long-Term Strategy:

Develop a long-term blockchain strategy aligned with the organization's overall digital transformation goals.

Stay informed about emerging trends and technologies in the blockchain space.

By following these steps and considerations, enterprises can increase the likelihood of successful blockchain implementation, fostering innovation, efficiency, and transparency within their operations.

Conclusion

Digital transformation and blockchain are two powerful forces that are revolutionizing the way we live, work, and do business. Digital transformation provides the tools and infrastructure that are needed to implement blockchain technologies. Blockchain, in turn, can provide new business opportunities and improve the efficiency and effectiveness of digital transformation initiatives.

Together, digital transformation and blockchain are creating a new world of possibilities for businesses. Businesses that are able to harness these technologies will be able to gain a competitive advantage and create new value for their customers.

Key takeaways

Digital transformation and blockchain are complementary and mutually reinforcing trends.

Blockchain can be used to address a wide range of challenges, including supply chain management, identity verification, and voting.

The future of blockchain is bright, with the potential to revolutionize many industries.

Business leaders should:

- Identify opportunities where blockchain can be applied to their operations.
- Develop a strategy for implementing blockchain technologies.
- Select the appropriate blockchain platform and tools.
- Implement blockchain in a phased approach.
- Train and upskill their workforce.
- Integrate blockchain with existing systems.
- Monitor and evaluate performance.

By taking these steps, businesses can position themselves for success in the digital transformation and blockchain era.

Meta (formerly Facebook): Meta's Diem stablecoin project, which aims to create a stablecoin that is backed by a basket of fiat currencies.

Microsoft: Microsoft's Azure Blockchain service, which allows businesses to build and deploy blockchain applications on Microsoft's cloud platform.

IBM: IBM's Hyperledger Fabric platform, which is a open-source blockchain framework for developing enterprise-grade blockchain applications.

Amazon: Amazon Web Services (AWS) Blockchain Templates, which are pre-built templates that make it easy to deploy and manage blockchain applications on AWS.

JPMorgan Chase: JPMorgan Chase's Quorum blockchain platform, which is a permissioned blockchain that is designed for enterprise use.

BlockFi: BlockFi's interest-earning accounts, which allow users to deposit cryptocurrencies and earn interest on their holdings.

Coinbase: Coinbase's cryptocurrency exchange, which allows users to buy, sell, and trade cryptocurrencies.

Paxos: Paxos's stablecoin products, which are stablecoins that are backed by fiat currencies or other assets.

Stellar: Stellar's blockchain network, which is a decentralized network for exchanging and trading digital assets.

These are just a few of the many companies that are working on blockchain technology. Blockchain is a rapidly growing field, and we can expect to see even more innovation in the coming years.

Digital Twins & Robotics

History of Digital Twins:

The concept of a digital twin traces its roots back to the 1960s when NASA used early forms of digital replicas to simulate and control spacecraft missions.

In the 1970s, the field of computer-aided design (CAD) and computer-aided engineering (CAE) laid the groundwork for digital twin technologies by creating virtual models for design and analysis.

The term "digital twin" was coined by Dr. Michael Grieves at the University of Michigan in 2002. He defined it as a virtual representation of a physical system that allows for monitoring, control, and optimization.

2010s: Rise of IoT and Industry 4.0

The emergence of the Internet of Things (IoT) and Industry 4.0 concepts significantly contributed to the development of digital twins.IoT sensors and devices began to generate vast amounts of real-time data from physical assets, providing the foundation for creating accurate and dynamic digital replicas.Industries such as manufacturing, healthcare, and energy started adopting digital twin technologies for predictive maintenance, process optimization, and simulation.

2017: General Acceptance and Growth

The term "digital twin" gained widespread acceptance, and major companies started implementing digital twin strategies.Siemens, a global industrial manufacturing company, played a pivotal role in promoting digital twins across various industries. They introduced their version of a comprehensive digital twin platform.

2018-2020: Integration with AI and Analytics

Integration with artificial intelligence (AI) and advanced analytics became a key trend. Digital twins started incorporating machine learning algorithms to enhance predictive capabilities.

Industries like aviation, automotive, and smart cities utilized digital twins for simulating and optimizing complex systems.

Present and Future: Expanding Applications

Digital twins continue to evolve with advancements in AI, machine learning, and 5G connectivity.

The technology is expanding into new areas, including smart buildings, agriculture, and urban planning, enabling more sophisticated simulations and optimizations.

Implementation of Digital Twins

Digital twins are typically implemented in a three-step process:

Data collection: The first step is to collect data from the physical object or system that is being represented by the digital twin. This data can come from a variety of sources, such as sensors, IoT devices, and existing databases.

Data modeling: The second step is to model the data collected in the first step. This involves creating virtual representations of the physical object or system. The models can be used to simulate the behavior of the object or system and to predict its performance.

Real-time updating: The third step is to update the digital twin in real time with new data from the physical object or system. This ensures that the digital twin is always up-to-date and reflects the current state of the physical object or system.

Future of Digital Twins

Digital twins are expected to play an increasingly important role in a variety of industries, including:

Manufacturing: Digital twins can be used to optimize production processes, improve product quality, and reduce downtime.

Supply chain management: Digital twins can be used to track the movement of goods and materials through the supply chain, identify and prevent disruptions, and optimize delivery routes.

Healthcare: Digital twins can be used to model the human body and simulate the effects of treatments, develop new drugs and therapies, and improve patient care.

Energy: Digital twins can be used to model power grids and optimize energy distribution, improve grid reliability, and reduce carbon emissions.

Buildings: Digital twins can be used to model buildings and simulate their energy consumption, identify and fix energy leaks, and improve the comfort of occupants.

As digital twins become more sophisticated, they are expected to be used in even more innovative ways. For example, they could be used to develop self-driving cars, predict natural disasters, and optimize traffic flow.

Benefits of Digital Twins

There are a number of benefits to using digital twins, including:

Improved decision-making: Digital twins can be used to make better decisions about the design, operation, and maintenance of physical objects and systems.

Increased efficiency: Digital twins can be used to improve the efficiency of operations by identifying and eliminating inefficiencies.

Reduced costs: Digital twins can be used to reduce costs by optimizing resource use and preventing downtime.

Improved safety: Digital twins can be used to improve safety by identifying potential hazards and preventing accidents.

Challenges of Digital Twins

There are also a number of challenges associated with using digital twins, including:

Data collection: Collecting and maintaining the data needed to create accurate digital twins can be a challenge.

Modeling: Modeling the behavior of physical objects and systems can be complex and time-consuming.

Integration: Integrating digital twins with existing systems can be a challenge.

Cost: Implementing and maintaining digital twins can be expensive.

Despite the challenges, the benefits of using digital twins are significant. As digital twins become more sophisticated and affordable, we can expect to see them being used in a wider range of industries and applications.

Siemens: Siemens' Xcelerator digital twin platform, which is a comprehensive suite of tools and services for developing, deploying, and managing digital twins.

Dassault Systèmes: Dassault Systèmes' 3DEXPERIENCE platform, which is a cloud-based platform that includes a digital twin capability.

PTC: PTC's ThingWorx platform, which is a platform for developing Internet of Things (IoT) applications that can include digital twin capabilities.

ABB: ABB's ABB Ability digital twin platform, which is a platform for developing industrial digital twins.

GE Digital: GE Digital's Predix platform, which is a platform for developing industrial IoT applications that can include digital twin capabilities.

Oracle: Oracle's Oracle Fusion Digital Twin, which is a digital twin platform that is part of Oracle's Fusion Applications suite.

SAP: SAP's SAP Leonardo Digital Twin, which is a digital twin platform that is part of SAP's Leonardo suite of cloud-based technologies.

Microsoft: Microsoft's Azure Digital Twins service, which is a cloud-based digital twin platform that is part of Microsoft's Azure cloud platform.

AWS IoT TwinMaker: AWS IoT TwinMaker is a fully managed service that helps you create, operate, and govern Digital Twin applications.

Google Cloud IoT: Google Cloud IoT is a fully managed service that helps you connect your IoT devices and gain insights from the data they generate.

IBM Watson IoT: IBM Watson IoT is a platform that helps you connect, manage, and analyze IoT data from devices, applications, and sensors.

Cisco IoT: Cisco IoT is a platform that helps you connect, manage, and secure IoT devices and data.

These are just a few of the many companies that are working on digital twins technology. Digital twins are a rapidly growing field, and we can expect to see even more innovation in the coming years.

History of Robotics:

Ancient Times: Early Automata

The concept of automation and basic forms of mechanical devices can be traced back to ancient civilizations. Examples include ancient Chinese mechanical puppets and Greek automatons.

1940s-1960s: Early Industrial Robots

The modern era of robotics began in the 1940s with the development of industrial robots. The Unimate, introduced in 1961, is considered the first industrial robot. It was used for tasks like loading and unloading heavy parts in a General Motors factory.

1970s-1980s: Expansion of Robotics in Manufacturing

The 1970s and 1980s saw a significant expansion of robotics in manufacturing industries. Robots were used for welding, painting, and assembly line tasks.

Companies like Fanuc and ABB emerged as leaders in industrial robotics.

1990s-2000s: Advances in Robotics Technology

Robotics technology advanced with the development of more sophisticated sensors, actuators, and control systems.

The medical field saw the introduction of robotic-assisted surgery systems like the da Vinci Surgical System.

2010s: Collaborative Robots and AI Integration

Collaborative robots (cobots) gained popularity, designed to work alongside humans in a shared workspace.

Integration with artificial intelligence and machine learning enabled robots to perform more complex tasks and adapt to changing environments.

Present and Future: Autonomous Systems and Humanoid Robots

The present landscape includes the rise of autonomous systems, drones, and robots capable of tasks in unstructured environments.Humanoid robots, designed to resemble and interact with humans, are being developed for various applications, including customer service and healthcare.

Continued Evolution: Emerging Technologies

Robotics continues to evolve with advancements in soft robotics, bio-inspired designs, and swarm robotics.Applications are expanding to areas like logistics, healthcare, and service industries, with an emphasis on human-robot collaboration.

The histories of digital twins and robotics intertwine with technological advancements, from early concepts to the present era of sophisticated, interconnected systems. As these technologies continue to progress, their combined impact is evident in the realms of automation, simulation, and the creation of intelligent, responsive environments.

Implementation of Robotics

The implementation of robotics involves a multi-step process that encompasses the design, development, testing, and deployment of robots. Here's a breakdown of the key stages involved:

Conceptual Design: The process begins with conceptualizing the desired function and capabilities of the robot. This involves identifying the specific task or application the robot will be designed for, considering the desired level of autonomy and maneuverability, and outlining the desired performance metrics.

Mechanical Design: The mechanical design phase focuses on the physical structure and components of the robot. This involves creating detailed CAD models, selecting materials, and designing the robot's joints, actuators, sensors, and end effectors.

Electronics and Control Design: The electronics and control design phase involves developing the electronic circuitry and software that will enable the robot to function autonomously or in response to external commands. This includes designing the robot's power supply, sensors, actuators, and control systems.

Programming and Simulation: The programming and simulation phase involves creating the software that will control the robot's behavior. This involves writing code that translates sensor data into actions, enabling the robot to perform the desired tasks. Simulations are also used to test the robot's performance and identify any potential problems before physical deployment.

Testing and Refinement: Once the robot has been designed and programmed, it undergoes rigorous testing to ensure its functionality, safety, and reliability. This may involve testing the robot in a controlled environment, such as a laboratory or factory, to validate its ability to perform the intended tasks.

Deployment and Integration: Once testing is complete, the robot is deployed into the target environment. This may involve integrating the robot with existing systems, such as conveyor belts, production lines, or healthcare equipment, and training operators on its operation and maintenance.

Future of Robotics

Robotics is a rapidly evolving field with the potential to revolutionize many industries and aspects of our lives. As the technology continues to develop, we can expect to see even more sophisticated robots with increased capabilities and autonomy.

Here are some of the key trends that are expected to shape the future of robotics:

Greater Autonomy: Robots are becoming increasingly autonomous, capable of making decisions and adapting to changing environments without human intervention.

Collaboration with Humans: Robots are being designed to work alongside humans in a more collaborative and safe manner.

Sensor Fusion: Robots are being equipped with advanced sensors that enable them to perceive and interact with their environment more effectively.

Learning and Adaption: Robots are being equipped with machine learning algorithms that allow them to learn and adapt to new situations.

Human-Robot Interaction (HRI): The development of natural language processing and other technologies is improving the ability of humans to interact with robots in a more natural and intuitive way.

These trends are leading to the development of robots that are more versatile, adaptable, and intelligent. This will enable them to take on a wider range of tasks, from manufacturing and healthcare to customer service and education. As robots become more integrated into our lives, we need to consider the ethical and societal implications of their use.

Companies that are working on robotics and their current projects:

- *Boston Dynamics* is developing a wide range of robots for a variety of applications, including Atlas, a humanoid robot that can walk, run, and climb; Spot, a quadruped robot that can be used for inspection and security; and Handle, a robot arm that can be used to manipulate objects.

- *Universal Robots* is developing a line of collaborative robots (cobots) that can work safely alongside humans. Cobots are becoming increasingly popular in manufacturing and other industries because they can automate tasks that are dangerous or repetitive for humans.

- *Rethink Robotics* is developing a line of robots for a variety of applications, including Baxter, a collaborative robot that can be used for light assembly and other tasks; and Sawyer, a collaborative robot that can be used for heavier-duty tasks

- *KUKA* is a German robotics company that is developing a wide range of robots for a variety of applications, including robots for industrial automation, robots for logistics and warehousing, and robots for healthcare.

- *Fanuc* is a Japanese robotics company that is developing a wide range of robots for a variety of applications, including robots for industrial automation, robots for aerospace and defense, and robots for automotive.

- *ABB* is a Swiss-Swedish multinational corporation that is developing a wide range of robots for a variety of applications, including robots for industrial automation, robots for power and utilities, and robots for packaging and handling.

- *Yaskawa Electric* is a Japanese multinational corporation that is developing a wide range of robots for a variety of applications, including robots for industrial automation, robots for material handling, and robots for welding.

- *Honda* is a Japanese multinational corporation that is developing a line of robots for a variety of applications, including robots for manufacturing, robots for logistics and warehousing, and robots for healthcare.

- *Mitsubishi Electric* is a Japanese multinational corporation that is developing a wide range of robots for a variety of applications, including robots for industrial automation, robots for assembly, and robots for welding.

- *iRobot* is an American corporation that is developing a line of robots for a variety of applications, including Roomba, a robotic vacuum cleaner; Scooba, a robotic mop; and Braava Jet, a robotic floor mopper.

These are just a few of the many companies that are working on robotics. Robotics is a rapidly growing field, and we can expect to see even more innovation in the coming years.

AR\VR\XR

History of AR\VR\XR

The concepts of augmented reality (AR), virtual reality (VR), and extended reality (XR) have been around for decades, but it is only in recent years that they have begun to gain widespread adoption.

Augmented Reality

The term "augmented reality" was coined by Tom Caudell and Ivan Sutherland in the 1990s. AR is a technology that overlays computer-generated images onto the real world, creating a blended experience.

The first commercial AR application was the Heads-Up Display (HUD) used in fighter jets in the 1990s. HUDs project important information, such as navigation data and enemy locations, onto the pilot's helmet, allowing them to see the information without taking their eyes off the sky.

In recent years, AR has become more accessible to consumers with the development of smartphones and tablets that have built-in AR capabilities. Apps like Pokémon Go and Snapchat have popularized AR, and it is now being used in a variety of applications, including gaming, education, and retail.

Virtual Reality

The concept of virtual reality was first proposed by Jaron Lanier in the 1980s. VR is a technology that creates a simulated environment that can be interacted with using headsets and other devices.

The first commercial VR headsets were developed in the 1990s, but they were bulky and expensive, and they did not have the processing power to create realistic experiences.

In recent years, VR has become more affordable and accessible with the development of lighter, more powerful headsets and the improvement of graphics processing capabilities. VR is now being used in a variety of applications, including gaming, entertainment, and training.

Extended Reality

Extended reality (XR) is an umbrella term that encompasses AR, VR, and other related technologies, such as mixed reality (MR). MR combines elements of AR and VR, creating a hybrid experience that allows users to interact with both the real and virtual worlds.

XR is still in its early stages of development, but it has the potential to revolutionize many industries, including healthcare, education, and manufacturing.

Future of AR\VR\XR

The future of AR, VR, and XR is bright. These technologies are expected to become even more sophisticated, affordable, and accessible in the coming years.

Improved hardware: Headsets are becoming lighter, more comfortable, and more powerful.

More realistic graphics: Graphics are becoming more realistic and immersive.

Increased interactivity: Users will be able to interact with virtual objects in more natural and intuitive ways.

More applications: AR, VR, and XR are being used in a wider range of applications, including gaming, education, and training.

Ubiquitous computing: AR, VR, and XR will become more integrated into our daily lives.

As AR, VR, and XR continue to evolve, they will have a profound impact on how we work, live, and play.

*Leading companies in the AR, VR, and XR space
and their current projects:*

Meta (formerly Facebook):

Project Cambria: Meta's next-generation VR headset that is expected to offer higher resolution, better eye-tracking, and more realistic graphics.

Project Nazare: Meta's AR glasses that are expected to provide a more seamless and immersive AR experience.

Meta Horizon Worlds: Meta's social VR platform that allows users to create and explore virtual worlds with other people.

Apple:

Apple Glasses: Apple's rumored AR glasses that are expected to offer a range of augmented reality features for everyday tasks.

Apple AR/VR SDK: Apple's software development kit (SDK) that allows developers to create AR and VR experiences for iOS and macOS devices.

Apple's Reality Composer: Apple's prototyping tool that allows developers to create and test AR experiences without writing any code.

Microsoft:

Microsoft Mesh: Microsoft's collaborative mixed reality platform that allows users to interact with each other and virtual objects in real-time.

Microsoft Azure Spatial Anchors: Microsoft's cloud-based technology that allows developers to place virtual objects in the real world and share them with others.

Microsoft HoloLens 2: Microsoft's most advanced AR headset that is designed for enterprise use.

Niantic:

Pokémon Go Beyond: Niantic's continued development of the popular AR game Pokémon Go, including new features and updates.

Peridot: Niantic's new AR game that is designed for social interactions and exploration.

Lightship SDK: Niantic's software development kit (SDK) that allows developers to create AR experiences for mobile devices.

Spectacles 4: Snap Inc.'s latest version of its AR glasses that offer improved performance and new features.

Snapchat AR Lenses: Snap Inc.'s continued development of creative AR lenses for its Snapchat app.

Snapverse: Snap Inc.'s vision for a social metaverse that combines AR, VR, and other technologies.

Enlight: Pursuit of Value

"Future-proofing" in digital transformation refers to the process of ensuring that a company's digital initiatives are sustainable and adaptable to the ever-changing technological landscape. This includes building a resilient infrastructure, adopting emerging technologies, and fostering a culture of innovation.

Building a Resilient Infrastructure: A resilient infrastructure is essential for supporting a company's digital transformation efforts. This includes:

Securing data and systems: Protecting sensitive data and ensuring that systems are up to date and patched is crucial for preventing cyberattacks and data breaches.

Embracing cloud computing: Cloud computing offers scalability, flexibility, and cost-effectiveness, making it an ideal platform for digital transformation.

Investing in IT infrastructure: Regularly upgrading hardware and software is essential to ensure that the infrastructure can support the company's growing digital needs.

Adopting Emerging Technologies Staying ahead of the curve by adopting emerging technologies is essential for future-proofing a company's digital transformation. This includes:

Artificial intelligence (AI): AI is transforming industries across the board, from healthcare to manufacturing. Businesses should explore how AI can be applied to their operations to improve efficiency, customer service, and decision-making.

Internet of Things (IoT): The IoT connects physical devices to the internet, enabling data collection and real-time insights. Businesses should identify opportunities to leverage IoT to improve operations, enhance customer experiences, and gain competitive advantage.

Blockchain: Blockchain is a distributed ledger technology that can be used to create secure, transparent, and tamper-proof records. Businesses should explore how blockchain can be used to streamline processes, manage supply chains, and build trust with customers.

Fostering a Culture of Innovation A culture of innovation is essential for driving a company's digital transformation journey. This includes:Encouraging experimentation: Fostering a culture of experimentation allows employees to test new ideas and learn from failures.

Empowering employees: Giving employees ownership and autonomy over digital initiatives can unleash innovation.

Celebrating success: Recognizing and rewarding employees for their contributions to digital initiatives can encourage further innovation. By investing in a resilient infrastructure, adopting emerging technologies, and fostering a culture of innovation, companies can future-proof their digital transformation efforts and remain competitive in an ever-evolving technological landscape.

Building a resilient digital company requires a comprehensive approach that encompasses people, processes, and technology. Here are some key steps to consider:

Establish a Strong Leadership Commitment:

Top-level leadership must be fully committed to the digital transformation journey and provide unwavering support for its implementation. This includes allocating resources, setting clear expectations, and fostering a culture of innovation and collaboration.

Create a Culture of Data-Driven Decision-Making:

Data is the cornerstone of a resilient digital company. Invest in data management and analytics capabilities to collect, analyze, and derive insights from the vast amounts of data generated by your digital operations. Use these insights to inform decision-making, optimize processes, and enhance customer experiences.

Prioritize Security and Privacy:

Cybersecurity is paramount for protecting your digital assets, customer data, and reputation. Implement robust security measures, including data encryption, strong authentication, and regular security audits, to safeguard your digital infrastructure from cyberattacks and data breaches.

Foster a Collaborative and Experimentation-Driven

Embrace a culture of experimentation where employees feel empowered to test new ideas, learn from failures, and continuously improve. Encourage cross-functional collaboration to break down silos and accelerate innovation.

Invest in a Resilient and Scalable Infrastructure:

Ensure your digital infrastructure can handle fluctuating workloads, spikes in traffic, and evolving business requirements. Invest in scalable and robust cloud-based solutions that can adapt seamlessly to changing needs.

Upskill and Reskill Employees for the Digital Age:

Invest in employee training and upskilling to equip them with the necessary skills and knowledge to navigate the digital transformation journey. Provide opportunities for digital learning and development to empower employees to embrace new technologies and adapt to change.

Cultivate a Customer-Centric Approach:

Prioritize customer needs, preferences, and behaviors in all aspects of your digital strategy. Personalize experiences, provide seamless interactions, and address customer concerns promptly to foster loyalty and advocacy.

Continuously Monitor and Adapt:

Regularly assess the performance of your digital initiatives and make adjustments as needed. Use data and analytics to identify areas for improvement, optimize processes, and enhance customer experiences.

Embrace Agility and Continuous Improvement:

Adopt agile development methodologies to adapt quickly to changing market conditions and customer needs. Embrace continuous improvement practices to continuously refine and optimize your digital solutions.

Collaborate with Partners and Ecosystems:

Expand your reach and expertise by collaborating with complementary companies and organizations. Build strategic partnerships to leverage new technologies, resources, and market insights.

Building a resilient digital company is an ongoing process that requires continuous adaptation, innovation, and learning. By incorporating these key steps into your digital transformation journey, you can create a company that is future-proof and prepared to thrive in the ever-evolving digital landscape.

Human Factor

People are the foundation of any successful digital transformation initiative. Without the right people, it is impossible to effectively implement new technologies, change processes, and achieve the desired outcomes. Here are some of the key reasons why people are so important in digital transformation:

People are the ones who use and adopt new technologies.

Digital transformation is not just about deploying new tools and platforms; it's about creating a culture where employees are comfortable using and adopting these technologies. To do that, you need to invest in training, support, and change management to ensure that people are up-to-date on the latest technologies and feel empowered to use them effectively.

People are the ones who drive innovation.

Digital transformation is not just about automating tasks; it's also about creating new products, services, and business models. To do that, you need to tap into the creativity and ingenuity of your employees. Encourage experimentation, collaboration, and risk-taking to foster a culture of innovation.

People are the ones who deliver value to customers.

At the end of the day, digital transformation is about improving the customer experience. And that ultimately comes down to the people who interact with customers on a daily basis. Invest in training, coaching, and empowerment so that your employees can provide exceptional customer service.

In today's digital age, trust is more important than ever. And that trust is built on the relationships between people. Invest in employee engagement, communication, and feedback to create a positive and supportive work environment where employees feel valued and respected.By putting people first, you can create a successful digital transformation that drives innovation, improves customer experience, and builds trust and loyalty.

The human factor plays a critical role in the success of digital transformation initiatives. It encompasses the attitudes, skills, collaboration, and adaptability of individuals within an organization. Effectively managing the human side of digital transformation is essential for ensuring that technology adoption aligns with organizational goals, and that employees are empowered and motivated throughout the process.

Key considerations regarding the human factor in digital transformation:

Leadership and Culture:

Leadership Buy-In: Leadership support and buy-in are crucial for driving a digital transformation. Leaders should champion the change, set the vision, and exemplify a commitment to innovation.

Cultural Alignment: Assess and align the organizational culture with the goals of digital transformation. A culture that values innovation, learning, and adaptability fosters a conducive environment for change.

Change Management:

Communication: Effective communication is essential to keep employees informed about the reasons behind the digital transformation, the benefits, and the expected changes.

Change Agents: Identify and empower change agents within the organization who can act as advocates, provide support, and guide their colleagues through the transformation journey.

Employee Engagement:

Inclusivity: Involve employees in the decision-making process. Solicit feedback, listen to concerns, and incorporate insights from those directly impacted by the changes.

Training and Upskilling: Provide training programs and resources to upskill employees in line with the new technologies being introduced. This enhances their confidence and ability to adapt.

User-Centric Design:

User Experience (UX):   Prioritize the user experience when implementing new digital tools or interfaces. A positive user experience contributes to user acceptance and minimizes resistance.

Feedback Loops: Establish feedback mechanisms to continuously gather user feedback, allowing for iterative improvements based on real user experiences.

Collaboration and Cross-Functional Teams:

Cross-Functional Collaboration: Encourage collaboration across different departments and functions. Cross-functional teams can provide diverse perspectives and contribute to innovative solutions.

Interdisciplinary Teams: Form interdisciplinary teams that bring together individuals with different skills and backgrounds to address complex challenges.

Digital Leadership Skills:

Digital Literacy: Foster digital literacy across all levels of the organization. This includes not only technical skills but also an understanding of the broader digital landscape.

Adaptability: Cultivate a culture of adaptability. Employees should feel empowered to learn and adapt to new technologies and methodologies as the digital landscape evolves.

Resilience and Agility:

Resilience Training: Provide training and support programs that help employees develop resilience in the face of change. Resilient teams are better equipped to navigate challenges.

Agile Mindset: Promote an agile mindset that encourages quick adaptation to changing circumstances and the ability to iterate on solutions.

Ethical Considerations:

Ethical Awareness: Educate employees about ethical considerations related to technology use. This includes privacy concerns, data security, and responsible AI practices.

Ethical Decision-Making: Empower employees to make ethical decisions by providing guidelines and fostering a culture of integrity.

Workplace Wellbeing:

Work-Life Balance: Prioritize work-life balance to prevent burnout. Digital transformation should enhance efficiency without negatively impacting employee wellbeing.

Mental Health Support: Offer resources and support for mental health, recognizing the potential stress associated with organizational change.

Feedback and Recognition:

Recognition Programs: Implement recognition programs to acknowledge and celebrate achievements related to digital transformation.

Continuous Feedback: Establish mechanisms for continuous feedback, allowing employees to share their experiences, insights, and suggestions for improvement.

Diversity and Inclusion:

Inclusive Policies: Ensure that digital transformation initiatives consider diversity and inclusion. This includes diverse perspectives in decision-making and creating inclusive digital solutions.

Bias Mitigation: Address and mitigate biases in algorithms and technologies to promote fair and inclusive outcomes.

Measuring Impact:

Key Performance Indicators (KPIs): Define and measure key performance indicators related to the human factor. This could include employee satisfaction, productivity, and the successful adoption of new technologies.

Continuous Improvement: Use data and feedback to drive continuous improvement in digital transformation strategies and their impact on the workforce.

Employee Empowerment:

Empowerment Programs: Develop programs that empower employees to take ownership of their roles in the digital transformation journey.

Autonomy: Provide a level of autonomy for employees to explore and contribute to innovative solutions within their roles.

Reskilling and Upskilling Programs:

Learning Opportunities: Establish reskilling and upskilling programs that provide continuous learning opportunities for employees.

Career Development: Align digital transformation efforts with career development paths, demonstrating a commitment to employee growth.

Community Building:

Digital Community Platforms: Create digital community platforms or forums where employees can share knowledge, ask questions, and collaborate on digital initiatives.

Peer Learning: Facilitate peer learning and mentorship programs to encourage knowledge transfer and skill development.

Innovation Culture:

Innovation Initiatives: Encourage innovation through dedicated initiatives, hackathons, or innovation challenges that involve employees at all levels.

Failure Tolerance: Foster a culture that tolerates and learns from failures, promoting experimentation and creative problem-solving.

Digital Wellbeing:

Digital Detox Initiatives: Introduce initiatives that promote digital detox and healthy technology usage practices.

Ergonomics: Consider the ergonomic aspects of digital tools and workspaces to support employee health and comfort.

Psychological Safety:

Open Communication: Create an environment of open communication where employees feel psychologically safe to express their opinions and concerns.

Leadership Accessibility: Ensure leadership accessibility and approachability, encouraging open dialogue about the challenges and opportunities associated with digital transformation.

Employee Retention Strategies:

Retention Programs: Develop strategies to retain key talent during and after the digital transformation process.

Career Pathing: Provide clear career paths and opportunities for growth within the organization

Adaptive HR Policies:

Flexible Policies: Review and adapt HR policies to accommodate the changing nature of work introduced by digital transformation, including flexible work arrangements and remote work policies.

Employee-Centric Policies: Ensure that policies are designed with an employee-centric approach, considering the wellbeing and needs of the workforce.

User Feedback in Technology Adoption:

User Involvement: Involve end-users early in the design and selection of new technologies, ensuring that the tools meet their needs.

User Acceptance Testing: Conduct user acceptance testing to gather feedback and address any usability issues before full implementation.

Digital Citizenship Programs:

Digital Citizenship Training: Provide training on digital citizenship to promote responsible and ethical behavior in the digital realm.

Cybersecurity Awareness: Increase awareness about cybersecurity practices and the importance of

Neglecting people in the process of digital transformation can have significant negative consequences for both individuals and the organization as a whole.

Potential outcomes of neglecting the human factor in digital transformation:

Resistance to Change:

Low Adoption Rates: Without proper consideration for the needs and concerns of employees, there is a higher likelihood of resistance to change.

Decreased Morale: Neglecting the human element may lead to a decrease in morale and a lack of enthusiasm for adopting new technologies.

Decreased Productivity:

Learning Curve Challenges: Insufficient training and support during the transition can result in a steep learning curve for employees, leading to decreased productivity.

Workflow Disruptions: Inadequate consideration of how digital tools integrate with existing workflows may cause disruptions, impacting efficiency.

Increased Turnover:

Employee Frustration: Neglecting employees' concerns and not providing adequate support can contribute to frustration and dissatisfaction.

Talent Drain: Employees who feel undervalued or overwhelmed by the changes may seek opportunities elsewhere, leading to talent drain.

Failure of Digital Projects:

Underutilized Technology: If users are not adequately trained or do not see the value in new technologies, there is a risk of underutilization or complete failure of digital projects.

Wasted Investments: Investments in technology may not yield the expected returns if the human element is overlooked.

Negative Impact on Innovation:

Lack of Employee Involvement: Innovation often stems from the diverse perspectives of employees. Neglecting employee involvement in the digital transformation process can hinder innovative thinking.

Missed Opportunities: Employees on the front lines may have valuable insights into operational efficiencies and customer needs, which could be overlooked.

Erosion of Trust:

Perceived Lack of Care: Neglecting the human side of digital transformation may be perceived as a lack of care for employees' well-being and concerns.

Erosion of Trust: Trust in leadership and the organization may erode, impacting the overall organizational culture.

Cultural Misalignment:

Cultural Resistance: Neglecting the existing organizational culture and values may lead to resistance against digital initiatives that are perceived as conflicting with established norms.

Misalignment with Values: A misalignment between the values of the organization and the digital transformation goals can create tension and a sense of disconnection.

Increased Stress and Burnout:

Overwhelming Changes: Rapid and overwhelming changes without proper support can contribute to stress and burnout among employees.

Mental Health Impacts: Neglecting mental health considerations during digital transformation can lead to increased anxiety and mental health challenges.

Customer Dissatisfaction:

Impact on Service Quality: If employees struggle with new technologies or are not adequately trained, it can affect the quality of customer service, leading to customer dissatisfaction.

Loss of Customer Trust: Consistent issues with technology implementation may erode customer trust in the organization's ability to deliver reliable services.

Missed Opportunities for Innovation:

Employee Ideas Ignored: Neglecting to involve employees in the innovation process may result in missed opportunities for creative solutions to business challenges.

Stagnation: Without a culture that encourages and values innovation, the organization may struggle to keep up with industry advancements.

Strained Team Dynamics:

Communication Breakdowns: Neglecting communication and transparency during the digital transformation process can lead to misunderstandings and breakdowns in team dynamics.

Silos and Fragmentation: Lack of collaboration and cross-functional communication can result in silos and fragmented workflows.

Loss of Competitive Edge:

Inability to Adapt: Failure to consider the human element may result in an inability to adapt quickly to changing market conditions.

Loss of Competitive Advantage: Competitors who prioritize both technology and the well-being of their people may gain a competitive advantage.

Data Security Risks:

Employee Negligence: Neglecting to educate employees on data security measures can lead to increased risks of data breaches due to negligence.

Insufficient Training: Without proper training, employees may unknowingly engage in behaviors that compromise data security.

Decreased Employee Satisfaction:

Job Dissatisfaction: Employees who feel neglected in the digital transformation process may experience job dissatisfaction.

Negative Organizational Perception: Negative perceptions about the organization's commitment to its workforce can spread, affecting the overall employer brand.

Regulatory Compliance Risks:

Lack of Awareness: Neglecting to educate employees on regulatory compliance requirements associated with new technologies may lead to inadvertent violations.

Legal Consequences: Non-compliance with regulations can result in legal consequences and damage the organization's reputation.

Ineffective Change Management:

Resistance and Pushback: A lack of emphasis on change management can result in increased resistance and pushback from employees.

Unaddressed Concerns: Employee concerns left unaddressed can escalate, hindering the smooth implementation of changes.

Poor Reputation and Brand Damage:

Negative Public Perception: The perception that an organization neglects its people during digital transformation can lead to negative publicity.

Brand Damage: A poor reputation as an employer and a brand that neglects its workforce can have long-term consequences on recruitment and customer trust.

Longer Adjustment Period:

Extended Adaptation Time: Neglecting to support employees during the transition can result in a longer adjustment period.

Delayed Benefits Realization: The organization may experience delays in realizing the anticipated benefits of digital transformation due to prolonged adaptation.

Missed Employee Feedback:

Untapped Insights: Neglecting to actively seek and incorporate employee feedback means missing out on valuable insights that could improve digital solutions.

Unaddressed Pain Points: Employee pain points and challenges may go unaddressed, leading to a less effective and efficient digital ecosystem.

Lack of Alignment with Business Goals:

Diverted Focus: Neglecting to align digital transformation with the broader business goals can result in a misallocation of resources and efforts.

Missed Strategic Opportunities: The organization may miss strategic opportunities for growth and competitiveness.

Mitigating the Risks:

To mitigate these risks, organizations should prioritize a holistic approach that considers both technological and human aspects of digital transformation. This includes comprehensive change management, ongoing communication, employee training and support, and a commitment to creating a positive and adaptive organizational culture. Successful digital transformation requires a balanced focus on technology and the people who drive its implementation and utilization.

Banking & Finance

The future of digital transformation in banking and finance is marked by continued innovation, enhanced customer experiences, and the integration of advanced technologies. Here are some key trends and future-forward aspects in the digital transformation landscape for the banking and finance sector:

AI and Advanced Analytics:

Personalized Customer Experiences: AI-driven analytics will enable banks to offer highly personalized and context-aware experiences for customers.

Predictive Insights: Advanced analytics will be used for predictive modeling, allowing banks to anticipate customer needs, identify trends, and manage risks more effectively.

Open Banking and APIs:

Ecosystem Collaboration: Open banking will foster collaboration between traditional banks and third-party financial service providers, leading to the creation of innovative financial ecosystems.

API Integration: APIs will play a central role in facilitating seamless integration between different financial services, allowing customers to access a wide range of products and services through a single platform.

Blockchain and Digital Currencies:

Decentralized Finance (DeFi): Blockchain technology will underpin the growth of decentralized finance, enabling peer-to-peer transactions, smart contracts, and more.

Central Bank Digital Currencies (CBDCs): Some countries may explore or implement central bank-backed digital currencies, offering a new form of digital payment.

Cybersecurity and Fraud Prevention:

Behavioural Biometrics: Enhanced authentication methods, including behavioural biometrics, will be deployed to strengthen security and reduce the risk of unauthorized access.

AI-Powered Threat Detection: AI will play a crucial role in identifying and mitigating cybersecurity threats, offering real-time threat detection and response.

Digital Identity Solutions:

Biometric Authentication: Digital identity verification will increasingly rely on biometric technologies such as facial recognition and fingerprint scanning.

Self-Sovereign Identity (SSI): Customers may have more control over their digital identities through SSI, allowing them to share information securely.

Robotic Process Automation (RPA) and Chatbots:

Automation of Routine Tasks: RPA will be used to automate repetitive and rule-based tasks, improving operational efficiency.

AI-Powered Chatbots: Chatbots equipped with natural language processing will provide instant customer support and assistance, enhancing the overall customer experience.

Quantum Computing:

Advanced Data Processing: Quantum computing has the potential to revolutionize data processing, enabling faster and more complex calculations for risk management, fraud detection, and optimization algorithms.

Enhanced Encryption: Quantum-resistant cryptography may be

adopted to secure sensitive financial data against potential threats posed by quantum computing.

Augmented and Virtual Reality (AR/VR):

Virtual Branches: AR/VR technologies may be employed to create virtual branches, providing customers with immersive digital banking experiences.

Remote Advisory Services: Virtual reality could enhance remote advisory services, allowing financial advisors to interact with clients in a more immersive and personalized way.

5G Technology:

Enhanced Connectivity: The widespread adoption of 5G technology will provide faster and more reliable connectivity, enabling quicker and more efficient digital transactions.

IoT Integration: 5G will facilitate the integration of Internet of Things (IoT) devices, contributing to the growth of smart banking and financial services.

RegTech (Regulatory Technology):

Automated Compliance: RegTech solutions will automate compliance processes, helping financial institutions adhere to regulatory requirements more efficiently.

Real-Time Monitoring: Real-time monitoring and reporting capabilities will assist organizations in staying compliant with evolving regulations.

Sustainability and ESG Integration:

Green Finance Initiatives: Financial institutions will increasingly focus on sustainable and environmentally friendly finance initiatives, aligning with Environmental, Social, and Governance (ESG) principles.

Data Analytics for ESG Reporting: Advanced analytics will be used to gather and analyze data related to ESG criteria for better decision-making.

Asset Tokenization: Non-fungible tokens (NFTs) and tokenization will be explored for representing and trading digital and physical assets.

Digital Ownership: Ownership of financial assets and products may be represented digitally through blockchain-based tokens.

AI-Augmented Decision-Making: Financial professionals will increasingly collaborate with AI systems to make more informed decisions.

Ethical AI Practices: Emphasis on ethical AI practices will ensure responsible and transparent use of AI in financial decision-making.

Blockchain for Cross-Border Transactions: Blockchain technology will streamline cross-border payments, reducing processing times and costs.

Cryptocurrency Integration: Some financial institutions may explore using cryptocurrencies for cross-border transactions and remittances.

Automated Contract Execution: Smart contracts on blockchain platforms will automate the execution of financial agreements, reducing the need for intermediaries.

Efficiency and Transparency: Smart contracts enhance efficiency, transparency, and trust in financial transactions.

Privacy-Centric Solutions: Financial institutions will continue to invest in privacy-centric solutions to safeguard customer data.

Ethical Use of Data: There will be a heightened focus on ethical data practices, ensuring that customer data is used responsibly and transparently.

Fintech Collaboration:

Collaborative Partnerships: Traditional financial institutions will increasingly collaborate with fintech startups to leverage innovative technologies and enhanceservice offerings.

Fintech Ecosystems: Integrated fintech ecosystems will emerge, offering a range of financial services through partnerships and seamless integrations.

Real-Time Payments:

Instant Payment Systems: Real-time payment systems will become more prevalent, allowing for instant fund transfers between accounts.

24/7 Availability: Financial institutions will provide continuous, 24/7 availability of payment services, improving customer convenience.

Distributed Finance (DeFi):

Decentralized Lending and Borrowing: DeFi platforms will continue to expand, offering decentralized lending, borrowing, and other financial services.

Smart Contracts for Finance: Smart contracts on blockchain networks will power various DeFi applications, eliminating the need for traditional intermediaries.

Biometric Payment Authentication:

Biometric Payment Solutions: Biometric authentication methods, such as fingerprint and facial recognition, will play a key role in secure and convenient payment processes.

Contactless Transactions: Biometric authentication will enhance the security of contactless transactions, reducing reliance on traditional payment methods.

Conclusion:

The future of digital transformation in banking and finance is dynamic and multifaceted, driven by a continuous quest for innovation, improved efficiency, and enhanced customer experiences. The successful adaptation to these future-forward trends will depend on the agility and strategic vision of financial institutions as they navigate the evolving landscape of technology and consumer expectations.

Problem: Traditional loan underwriting processes are often manual and time-consuming, which can lead to delays in approving loans and missed opportunities for customers. Additionally, these processes may not be able to fully capture the nuances of each customer's financial situation, which can result in suboptimal loan decisions.

Solution: AI-powered loan underwriting tools can analyze vast amounts of customer data, including financial transactions, credit history, and social media activity, to make more informed and personalized lending decisions. These tools can identify patterns and anomalies that may not be apparent to human underwriters, which can help to reduce risk and improve loan approvals.

Benefits:

Faster loan application processing: AI can automate many of the steps in the underwriting process, which can significantly reduce the time it takes to approve loans.

More accurate loan decisions: AI can analyze more data and identify patterns that humans may miss, which can lead to more accurate loan decisions and reduced risk.

More personalized loan offers: AI can tailor loan offers to each customer's individual needs and financial situation, which can lead to increased customer satisfaction and loyalty.

EXAMPLES OF HOW AI-POWERED LOAN UNDERWRITING TOOLS ARE BEING USED:

HSBC: HSBC is using AI to automate credit card applications and approvals, which has led to a 30% reduction in processing time.

Bank of America: Bank of America is using AI to identify potential loan applicants who are at risk of default, which allows the bank to offer them additional support or deny their loan applications.

JPMorgan Chase: JPMorgan Chase is using AI to analyze customer spending patterns to identify potential fraud, which has led to a 10% reduction in fraud losses.

AI-powered fraud detection

Traditional fraud detection methods often rely on rule-based systems that can be easily bypassed by sophisticated fraudsters. AI, on the other hand, can analyze vast amounts of data, including customer behavior, transaction patterns, and device characteristics, to identify anomalies and potential fraud. This can help banks to detect and prevent fraud more effectively, which can save them money and protect their customers.

Example: Deutsche Bank is using AI to analyze customer spending patterns to identify potential fraud. The bank has seen a 10% reduction in fraud losses as a result of this initiative.

Personalized financial advice

AI can be used to provide personalized financial advice to customers. By analyzing customer data, AI can identify their financial goals, risk tolerance, and spending habits. This information can then be used to recommend tailored financial products, such as investment portfolios, savings plans, and debt management solutions.

Example: Fidelity Investments is using AI to provide personalized investment advice to its customers. The AI system analyzes customer data and market conditions to recommend the best investment options for each customer.

Virtual financial assistants

Virtual financial assistants (VFAs) are AI-powered chatbots that can provide customer service, answer questions, and complete transactions. VFA can be accessed through a bank's website or mobile app, and they can be used to handle a variety of tasks, such as account inquiries, bill payments, and loan applications.

Example: HSBC is using VFA to provide customer service for its mobile banking app. The VFA can answer questions about account balances, transactions, and fees, and it can also help customers to set up new accounts and manage their finances.

These are just a few examples of how digital transformation is being used to change the banking and finance industry. As technology continues to evolve, we can expect to see even more innovative use cases emerge in the years to come.

Healthcare

Digital transformation is rapidly transforming the healthcare industry, creating new opportunities to improve patient care, enhance operational efficiency, and reduce costs. Here are some key trends driving digital transformation in healthcare:

The rise of telemedicine and telehealth: The COVID-19 pandemic accelerated the adoption of telemedicine, allowing patients to connect with healthcare providers remotely through video conferencing and other technologies. Telemedicine is now being used for a wide range of services, including virtual consultations, remote monitoring, and chronic disease management.

The adoption of artificial intelligence (AI) and machine learning (ML): AI and ML are being used to automate tasks, improve diagnosis, and develop new treatments. AI-powered algorithms can analyze vast amounts of medical data to identify patterns and insights that may not be apparent to human experts. This can help to improve the accuracy of diagnoses, personalize treatment plans, and identify new drug targets.

The use of wearable devices and sensors: Wearable devices and sensors are being used to collect real-time data on patients' health, which can then be used to monitor chronic conditions, track exercise and fitness, and identify early signs of disease. This data can also be used to provide personalized health coaching and interventions.

The development of virtual reality (VR) and augmented reality (AR): VR and AR are being used to create immersive training experiences for healthcare professionals, provide patients with a more realistic understanding of their conditions, and offer new therapies for pain management and rehabilitation.

The use of blockchain technology: Blockchain is being used to create secure and transparent healthcare records, which can improve patient care coordination and reduce the risk of fraud. Blockchain can also be used to track the movement of medications and ensure that they are used safely and effectively.

Key benefits of digital transformation in healthcare: Improved patient care:

Digital technologies can enable more personalized and effective care, including remote monitoring, early diagnosis, and precision medicine.

Enhanced operational efficiency: Digital tools can streamline processes, automate tasks, and improve communication, leading to faster and more efficient care delivery.

Reduced costs: Digital technologies can help to reduce administrative costs, eliminate unnecessary duplication of services, and improve the use of resources.

Examples of how digital transformation is being used in healthcare:

Virtual consultations: Patients can now connect with healthcare providers virtually for consultations, eliminating the need for in-person visits.

Remote patient monitoring: Healthcare providers can monitor patients remotely through wearable devices and sensors, enabling early detection of chronic conditions and complications.

AI-powered diagnostics: AI algorithms can analyze medical images and other data to identify potential diseases and anomalies, supporting more accurate diagnoses.

Digital health records: Electronic health records (EHRs) can provide a more comprehensive and accessible view of a patient's health history, improving coordination of care.

Personalized medicine: AI and other technologies can be used to identify genetic and other factors that may influence a patient's response to treatment, enabling more targeted and effective therapies.

Challenges of digital transformation in healthcare:

Data security and privacy: Healthcare providers must ensure that patient data is secure and private, as this information is highly sensitive.

Technology adoption and training: Healthcare professionals may need to be trained on new technologies to ensure they are used effectively and safely.

Integration with legacy systems: Integrating new digital technologies with existing healthcare systems can be a complex and time-consuming process.

Cost: Implementing digital transformation initiatives can be expensive, and there may be a need to balance the costs of technology with the potential benefits.

Despite these challenges, digital transformation is transforming the healthcare industry in a positive way, leading to better care, reduced costs, and improved efficiency. As technology continues to evolve, we can expect to see even more innovative applications of digital technologies in the future.

Digital transformation in healthcare involves the use of digital technologies to improve the delivery of healthcare services, enhance patient care, and optimize operational processes. Here's a comprehensive overview of digital transformation initiatives in healthcare:

Electronic Health Records (EHRs):

- Centralize and digitize patient health records for easy accessibility by healthcare providers.

  Benefits:

- Improved patient care coordination.

- Quick access to patient histories, medications, and treatment plans.

- Reduction of paperwork and manual record-keeping errors.

Telemedicine and Virtual Health:

- Enable remote patient consultations, diagnosis, and monitoring.

  Benefits:

- Increased access to healthcare, especially in remote areas.

- Reduced healthcare costs and travel time for patients.

- Efficient management of chronic conditions through remote monitoring.

Health Information Exchange (HIE):

- Facilitate the secure exchange of patient information among healthcare providers.

- Benefits:

- Improved care coordination among different healthcare entities.

- Timely access to critical patient data, leading to better-informed decision-making.

Digital Imaging and Diagnostics:

- Transition from film-based imaging to digital imaging technologies.

  Benefits:

- Faster image processing and retrieval.

- Enhanced diagnostic accuracy.

- Improved collaboration among healthcare professionals for remote consultations.

Mobile Health (mHealth) Applications:

- Develop mobile applications for health monitoring, medication adherence, and wellness.

  Benefits:

- Empower patients to actively manage their health.

- Enable real-time data collection for healthcare providers.

- Support preventive care through health tracking.

Wearable Technology:

- Integrate wearable devices for continuous health monitoring.

  Benefits:

- Remote monitoring of vital signs.

- Early detection of health issues.

- Improved patient engagement in their health.

Artificial Intelligence (AI) in Healthcare:

- Implement AI for data analysis, diagnostics, and personalized medicine.

  Benefits:

- Faster and more accurate diagnosis.

- Predictive analytics for disease prevention.

- Customized treatment plans based on patient data.

Robotics in Surgery and Rehabilitation:

- Utilize robotic systems for surgery and rehabilitation processes.

  Benefits:

- Precision and minimally invasive surgeries.

- Enhanced physical therapy and rehabilitation.

- Remote surgery capabilities for expert consultations.

Data Analytics for Population Health Management:

- Analyze large datasets to identify trends, assess population health, and predict disease outbreaks.

  Benefits:

- Early identification of public health risks.

- Targeted interventions for at-risk populations.

- Efficient resource allocation based on health trends.

Blockchain in Healthcare:

- Ensure secure and interoperable sharing of healthcare data using blockchain technology.

  Benefits:

- Improved data security and integrity.

- Streamlined data sharing among healthcare entities.

- Patient-controlled access to health records.

Virtual Reality (VR) and Augmented Reality (AR):

- Use VR and AR for medical training, patient education, and therapy.
  Benefits:

- Immersive medical training experiences.

- Enhanced patient education and engagement.

- Therapeutic applications for pain management and mental health.

IoT in Healthcare:

- Connect medical devices and equipment to the internet for real-time monitoring.

- Benefits:

- Continuous monitoring of patient vitals.

- Timely alerts for abnormal conditions.

- Efficient management of medical equipment.

Genomics and Precision Medicine:

- Leverage genetic data for personalized treatment plans.

  Benefits:

- Tailored treatment approaches based on individual genetic makeup.

- Predictive risk assessments for certain conditions.

Chatbots and Virtual Assistants:

- Deploy AI-powered chatbots for patient interactions, appointment scheduling, and information retrieval.

  Benefits:

- Improved patient engagement.

- 24/7 availability for basic healthcare queries.

- Time and cost savings for administrative tasks.

Cybersecurity Measures:

- Implement robust cybersecurity measures to protect patient data.

  Benefits:

- Prevention of data breaches and unauthorized access.

- Maintenance of patient trust in digital healthcare services.

Challenges and Considerations:

Data Security and Privacy Concerns: Ensuring the confidentiality and privacy of patient data.

Interoperability: Achieving seamless integration and communication among diverse digital systems.

Regulatory Compliance: Adhering to healthcare regulations and standards.

Digital Divide: Addressing disparities in access to digital healthcare technologies.

In conclusion, digital transformation in healthcare is a multidimensional process that leverages technology to enhance patient care, improve operational efficiency, and drive innovation in the healthcare industry. The successful implementation of digital solutions requires careful consideration of data security, regulatory compliance, and the diverse needs of healthcare stakeholders.

Case study 1: IBM Watson for Oncology

IBM Watson for Oncology is a cloud-based AI platform that helps oncologists make more informed decisions about cancer treatment. The platform analyzes vast amounts of medical data, including patient records, clinical trials, and published research, to identify patterns and insights that may not be apparent to human experts. This information can help oncologists to personalize treatment plans, identify the most effective treatment options for each patient, and predict the likely outcomes of different treatment strategies.

Case study 2: Mayo Clinic's Virtual Care Program

The Mayo Clinic's Virtual Care Program offers a wide range of telemedicine services, including virtual consultations, remote monitoring, and chronic disease management. The program has been shown to improve patient satisfaction, reduce healthcare costs, and improve patient outcomes.

Case study 3: Apple's HealthKit and ResearchKit

Apple's HealthKit and ResearchKit are platforms that allow developers to create apps that integrate with Apple devices to collect and track health data. These apps can be used to monitor chronic conditions, track exercise and fitness, and provide personalized health coaching.

Case study 4: Welltok's Healthy Outcomes Platform

Welltok's Healthy Outcomes Platform is a cloud-based software that helps healthcare organizations improve population health. The platform uses data analytics to identify health risks, target interventions, and measure outcomes.

Case study 5: Novartis' digital twin platform

Novartis' digital twin platform uses AI to create a virtual representation of a patient's body. This virtual representation can be used to simulate the effects of different treatment options, predict the likely course of a patient's disease, and identify potential drug interactions.

These are just a few examples of how digital transformation is being used in healthcare. As technology continues to evolve, we can expect to see even more innovative applications of digital technologies in the future.

Supply chain

Digital transformation in the supply chain involves the integration of digital technologies and data-driven solutions to enhance visibility, efficiency, and collaboration across the entire supply chain ecosystem. Here are key components and initiatives in the digital transformation of the supply chain:

Digital Supply Chain Visibility:

Objective:

- Provide real-time visibility into the entire supply chain from sourcing to delivery.

Technologies:

- IoT (Internet of Things), RFID (Radio-Frequency Identification), sensors.

Benefits:

- Improved tracking and monitoring of goods in transit.
- Enhanced responsiveness to disruptions and delays.

Advanced Analytics and Predictive Analytics:

Objective:

- Utilize analytics for demand forecasting, inventory optimization, and risk management.

Technologies:

- Big Data analytics, machine learning.

Benefits:

- More accurate demand planning.

- Reduced excess inventory and carrying costs.

- Early identification and mitigation of supply chain risks.

Cloud-Based Supply Chain Management:

Objective:

- Transition from on-premise systems to cloud-based platforms for flexible and scalable supply chain management.

Technologies:

- Cloud computing, Software-as-a-Service (SaaS).

Benefits:

- Improved accessibility and collaboration among supply chain partners.

- Cost savings on infrastructure and maintenance.

Blockchain in Supply Chain:

Objective:

- Enhance transparency, traceability, and security in the supply chain by leveraging blockchain technology.

Technologies:

- Distributed ledger technology.

Benefits:

- Immutable and transparent record-keeping.

- Reduced fraud and counterfeit risks.

- Streamlined documentation processes.

Autonomous and Connected Vehicles:

Objective:

- Integrate autonomous and connected vehicles for efficient and reliable transportation.

Technologies:

- IoT, telematics, autonomous vehicles.

Benefits:

- Real-time tracking and monitoring of vehicle status.
- Improved route optimization and fuel efficiency.
- Reduced lead times and transportation costs.

Digital Twin Technology:

Objective:

- Create digital replicas of physical assets, products, and processes for simulation and analysis.

Technologies:

- IoT, simulation software.

Benefits:

- Virtual testing and optimization of supply chain processes.
- Improved decision-making through real-time insights.

Collaborative Platforms and Ecosystems:

Objective:

- Foster collaboration among supply chain partners through digital platforms.

Technologies:

- Collaborative platforms, B2B integration.

Benefits:

- Seamless communication and data exchange among partners.
- Enhanced coordination and responsiveness.

Robotic Process Automation (RPA):

Objective:

- Automate routine and rule-based tasks in supply chain processes.

Technologies:

- RPA, robotic systems.

Benefits:

- Increased efficiency and accuracy in data entry and processing.

- Cost savings through labor reduction in repetitive tasks.

3D Printing/Additive Manufacturing:

Objective:

- Integrate 3D printing for on-demand and localized manufacturing.

Technologies:

- 3D printing, additive manufacturing.

Benefits:

- Reduced lead times and transportation costs.
- Customization and flexibility in production.

10. Supplier Relationship Management (SRM) Systems:

Objective:

- Strengthen relationships with suppliers through digital platforms.

Technologies:

- SRM software, supplier portals.

Benefits:

- Improved collaboration and communication with suppliers.
- Enhanced visibility into supplier performance and risks.

11. Smart Warehousing and Inventory Management:

Objective:

- Implement smart technologies for efficient warehouse operations and inventory control.

Technologies:

- IoT, RFID, warehouse management systems.

Benefits:

- Real-time tracking of inventory levels.
- Reduced stockouts and overstock situations.

Objective:

- Digitize and streamline the procurement process.

Technologies:

- e-Procurement platforms, automation.

Benefits:

- Faster procurement cycles.

- Improved accuracy and transparency in procurement transactions.

Objective:

- Incorporate digital tools to measure and improve the sustainability of the supply chain.

Technologies:

- Sustainability analytics, IoT for environmental monitoring.

Benefits:

- Reduced environmental impact.

- Enhanced corporate reputation and compliance.

Objective:

- Enable real-time data processing at the edge of the network for faster decision-making.

Technologies:

- Edge computing, edge analytics.

Benefits:

- Reduced latency in data processing.

- Enhanced responsiveness to real-time events.

Challenges and Considerations:

---

*Data Security and Privacy:*Protecting sensitive supply chain data from cyber threats.

*Integration Complexity:*Ensuring seamless integration of diverse digital technologies and systems.

*Change Management:*Managing the cultural and organizational changes associated with digital transformation.

Skill Gaps: Developing the necessary skills and expertise for managing digital supply chain technologies.

Interoperability: Ensuring compatibility and interoperability among different digital solutions used by supply chain partners.

In summary, digital transformation in the supply chain is a strategic imperative for organizations aiming to optimize their operations, enhance collaboration, and respond more effectively to the dynamic challenges of the modern business environment. The successful implementation of digital supply chain initiatives requires a holistic approach that addresses technological, organizational, and process-related considerations.

Case study 1: Zara's real-time demand forecasting

Zara, a Spanish multinational clothing retailer, uses data analytics and AI to forecast demand for its products in real time. This allows the company to adjust its production and inventory levels accordingly, minimizing the risk of stockouts and overstocks. As a result, Zara can deliver the latest fashion trends to its customers more quickly and efficiently.

Case study 2: UPS's route optimization using dynamic routing

UPS, a global logistics company, uses AI algorithms to optimize delivery routes. This helps the company to save time and fuel, which can reduce costs and improve customer satisfaction. UPS's dynamic routing system takes into account traffic patterns, weather conditions, and other factors to create the most efficient routes for its drivers.

Case study 3: GE Aviation's predictive maintenance using IoT devices

GE Aviation, a division of General Electric that manufactures aircraft engines, uses IoT devices to monitor the condition of its engines. This data is used to predict potential failures, which allows GE to schedule maintenance proactively. This can help to prevent costly downtime and ensure that GE's engines are always in top working condition.

Case study 4: Walmart's blockchain-based supply chain traceability

Walmart, a multinational retail corporation, uses blockchain technology to track the movement of goods through its supply chain. This helps to ensure that products are authentic and that they meet Walmart's quality standards. Blockchain also helps to improve traceability, which can help Walmart to identify and address problems quickly.

Case study 5: Nestle's use of augmented reality (AR) for quality control

Nestle, a Swiss multinational food and beverage company, uses AR to train its employees on quality control procedures. AR headsets allow employees to see instructions and guidance overlaid on the real world, which can help them to perform their jobs more efficiently and accurately.

These are just a few examples of how digital transformation is being used to improve the efficiency, visibility, and resilience of supply chains. As technology continues to evolve, we can expect to see even more innovative applications of digital technologies in the future.

Retail

Digital transformation in the retail sector involves leveraging digital technologies to enhance the overall customer experience, optimize operations, and stay competitive in a rapidly evolving market. Here are key components and initiatives in the digital transformation of the retail industry:

E-Commerce and Online Marketplaces:

Objective:

- Establish and optimize online platforms for product sales and customer interactions.

Technologies:

- E-commerce platforms, mobile apps.

Benefits:

- Expanded market reach.
- Increased convenience for customers.
- Enhanced sales and revenue.

Omnichannel Retailing:

Objective:

- Integrate online and offline channels to provide a seamless shopping experience.

Technologies:

- Point-of-sale (POS) systems, inventory management software.

Benefits:

- Consistent customer experience across channels.
- Improved inventory visibility and management.
- Enhanced customer loyalty.

Contactless Payments:

Objective:

- Adopt and promote contactless payment methods for in-store and online transactions.

Technologies:

- NFC (Near Field Communication), mobile wallets.

Benefits:

- Faster and more convenient transactions.
- Enhanced payment security.
- Alignment with changing consumer preferences.

Personalized Marketing:

Objective:

- Utilize customer data to deliver personalized marketing messages and offers.

Technologies:

- Customer relationship management (CRM), data analytics.

Benefits:

- Improved customer engagement.
- Higher conversion rates.
- Increased customer loyalty.

Data Analytics and Business Intelligence:

Objective:

- Analyze data to gain insights into customer behavior, preferences, and market trends.

Technologies:

- Big Data analytics, business intelligence tools.

Benefits:

- Informed decision-making.

- Optimization of inventory and pricing strategies.

- Identification of market trends and opportunities.

Augmented Reality (AR) and Virtual Reality (VR):

Objective:

- Implement AR and VR technologies for virtual try-ons, product visualization, and immersive shopping experiences.

Technologies:

- AR/VR applications, smart mirrors.

Benefits:

- Enhanced customer engagement.

- Reduced product return rates.

- Innovative in-store experiences.

Supply Chain Visibility:

Objective:

- Enhance visibility and traceability in the supply chain to optimize inventory management.

Technologies:

- IoT, RFID, supply chain management systems.

Benefits:

- Reduced out-of-stock situations.

- Efficient order fulfillment.

- Improved demand forecasting.

AI-Powered Chatbots and Virtual Assistants:

Objective:

- Implement AI-driven chatbots for customer support, order tracking, and information retrieval.

Technologies:

- Natural language processing (NLP), AI chatbots.

Benefits:

- 24/7 customer support.

- Faster query resolution.

- Cost-effective customer service.

Smart Retail Stores:

Objective:

- Integrate smart technologies for in-store automation, inventory tracking, and personalized shopping experiences.

Technologies:

- IoT sensors, smart shelves, beacons.

Benefits:

- Enhanced in-store efficiency.

- Personalized shopping recommendations.

- Improved operational insights.

Subscription Models and Loyalty Programs:

Objective:

- Implement subscription-based models and loyalty programs to retain and reward customers.

Technologies:

- Customer loyalty platforms, subscription management systems.

Benefits:

- Increased customer retention.

- Higher customer lifetime value.

- Enhanced brand loyalty.

Voice Commerce:

Objective:

- Enable voice-activated shopping through virtual assistants and voice-enabled devices.

Technologies:

- Voice recognition, natural language processing.

Benefits:

- Streamlined shopping experiences.

- Increased accessibility.

- Simplified order processes.

Social Commerce:

Objective:

- Leverage social media platforms for direct sales and customer engagement.

Technologies:

- Social commerce features, influencer marketing.

Benefits:

- Direct product discovery and purchasing.

- Enhanced brand visibility and engagement.

- Social proof for products.

Dynamic Pricing:

Objective:

- Implement dynamic pricing strategies based on real-time market conditions and customer behavior.

Technologies:

- Machine learning algorithms, pricing optimization tools.

Benefits:

- Maximization of revenue.

- Competitive pricing strategies.

- Improved profitability.

Cybersecurity Measures:

Objective:

- Implement robust cybersecurity measures to protect customer data and online transactions.

Technologies:

- Encryption, secure payment gateways.

Benefits:

- Customer trust and confidence.
- Prevention of data breaches and cyber threats.

Environmental Sustainability:

Objective:

- Integrate sustainability practices in the supply chain and retail operations.

Technologies:

- Sustainability analytics, eco-friendly packaging.

Benefits:

- Enhanced corporate social responsibility.
- Attraction of environmentally conscious customers.

Challenges and Considerations:

Data Privacy and Security: Safeguarding customer data from cyber threats and ensuring compliance with data protection regulations.

Legacy System Integration: Addressing challenges associated with integrating new digital technologies with existing legacy systems.

Consumer Adoption: Encouraging and facilitating the adoption of digital tools and platforms by consumers.

Talent and Skill Gaps: Developing the necessary skills and expertise among retail staff to manage and leverage digital technologies.

Competitive Landscape: Staying agile and innovative to keep up with rapidly evolving market trends and competitor initiatives.

In summary, digital transformation in retail is a strategic imperative for staying competitive and meeting the evolving expectations of tech-savvy consumers. Successful digital transformation initiatives require a customer-centric approach, technological innovation, and a willingness to adapt to the changing landscape of retail.

Use cases of digital transformation

Case study 1: Amazon Go's cashier less checkout experience

Amazon Go is a grocery store chain that uses computer vision and other technologies to allow customers to shop without waiting in line to checkout. Customers simply scan their smartphones at the entrance to enter the store and then take the items they want. When they are finished shopping, they simply leave the store, and their purchases are automatically charged to their Amazon account.

Case study 2: Sephora's Virtual Try-On with augmented reality (AR)

Sephora is a cosmetics retailer that uses AR to allow customers to virtually try on makeup products before they buy them. Customers can use the Sephora app to take a selfie, and then the app will apply different makeup looks to their face. This can help customers to find the perfect shade of foundation or lipstick, and it can also help them to avoid buying products that they will not like.

Case study 3: Nike's Hyper Adapt 1.0 self-lacing sneakers

Nike is a shoe manufacturer that uses robotics to create self-lacing sneakers. The Hyper Adapt 1.0 sneakers have sensors that detect the wearer's foot and tighten or loosen the laces accordingly. This can help to provide a more comfortable and personalized fit.

Case study 4: Alibaba's Hema Fresh grocery stores

Alibaba is an e-commerce company that uses AI and other technologies to create smart grocery stores. Hema Fresh stores use AI to recommend products to customers, to track inventory levels, and to automate the checkout process.

Case study 5: Macy's virtual reality fitting rooms

Macy's is a department store chain that is using VR to create virtual fitting rooms. Customers can use the Macy's app to create a 3D avatar of themselves, and then they can try on different clothes in the virtual fitting room. This can help customers to see how clothes will look on them before they buy them, and it can also help them to avoid buying clothes that will not fit them well.

These are just a few examples of how digital transformation is being used in retail. As technology continues to evolve, we can expect to see even more innovative applications of digital technologies in the retail sector.

Key takeaways:

Digital transformation is a critical imperative for businesses of all sizes and industries. It is not a one-time event, but an ongoing process of innovation and adaptation. There are many different ways to approach digital transformation, and there is no one-size-fits-all solution.

The key is to identify the right opportunities for digital transformation and develop a plan to implement them effectively.

Recommendations:

- Start small and build momentum. Don't try to transform your entire business overnight. Instead, start with a few small projects that can quickly deliver results.

- Get buy-in from leadership. Digital transformation requires the support of senior management to be successful.
- Educate and empower your workforce. Your employees need to be trained on new technologies and processes to ensure they are prepared for the digital transformation journey.
- Measure and track your progress. It is important to track your progress and measure the impact of your digital transformation initiatives.
- Be agile and adaptable. The digital landscape is constantly changing, so you need to be able to adapt your plans as needed.

The future of digital transformation:

The future of digital transformation is bright. As technology continues to evolve, we can expect to see even more innovative applications of digital technologies in businesses of all shapes and sizes. Organizations that are able to harness the power of digital transformation will be able to gain a competitive advantage.

In the closing chapters of "Digital Transformation: Navigating the Future," we have explored the pivotal role of digital awareness as a catalyst for individual adaptability in the face of emerging technologies. The book has illuminated the fact that, in an environment where digital fluency is increasingly vital, individuals equipped with knowledge and skills stand better poised to remain competitive and thrive.

Moreover, we delved into the notion that the acquisition of knowledge in emerging fields is not merely a pursuit of information but a strategic pathway to unlocking a myriad of opportunities. This acquisition becomes a powerful tool in addressing the multifaceted challenges presented by our dynamic digital landscape. The book has aimed to serve as a guide, emphasizing the importance of continuous learning and staying abreast of industry trends to harness the full potential of digital transformation.

In the final chapters, we arrive at the profound realization that embracing this digital reality extends beyond a strategic imperative; it is a testament to our collective belief. It is a belief that, ultimately, the strength of any transformative journey lies in the hands, minds, and hearts of the individuals who drive it. As organizations and individuals alike embark on this transformative path, it is not just about adopting cutting-edge technologies, but about fostering a mindset that welcomes change, innovation, and the power of collaboration.

In essence, the conclusion of this book encourages us to recognize that digital transformation is not solely a technological evolution; it is a human one. The true measure of success in the digital era lies not only in the tools we employ but in our ability to adapt, learn, and collaborate. As we close this chapter, let it be a call to action, urging each reader to embrace the reality of a digital future with open minds, resilient spirits, and a collective commitment to shaping a better tomorrow.